LONDON'S
DISUSED
UNDERGROUND
STATIONS

Acknowledgements

I would like to thank all of those who have helped in the production of this book, particularly Mike Ashworth, Peter Bancroft, Nick Catford, John Crook, Brian Hardy, David Leboff and my wife Tricia.

Photographic Credits

All photographs © London Transport Museum except those on pages:

J R Batts 12 bottom
P W Bradley 79 top
Capital Transport 31 top, 113 bottom
H C Casserley 96 lower
Nick Catford 14 both, 15, 18 both, 19 both, 20, 21 both, 26 bottom, 27 all, 32 both, 33 both, 34, 42 both, 43 both, 44, 45 top, 52 both, 53 both, 65 bottom, 67, 69 bottom, 120 both, 121 both, 122 both, 123
Commercial postcard 41 top, 90
J E Connor 13 bottom, 17, 26 top, 28 top, 35 all, 48, 72, 104, 105 bottom, 112 both, 113 top, 119 top, 128 bottom
J E Connor collection 4, 47 bottom, 56

R Collen-Jones 118 bottom
M Durrell collection 12 top, 51 lower right, 57 bottom
J C Gillham 128 top
Guildhall Library 7
M A C Horne 6
Justin Howes 40 top
Alan A Jackson 79 bottom
David Leboff 49 bottom, 105 top
LURS collection 40 bottom
Stations UK 109 top
Wilf Watters collection 9
Chris Wilson 124

ISBN 978-1-85414-467-6

Published by Capital Transport Publishing Ltd

www.capitaltransport.com

Printed by Parksons Graphics

LONDON'S DISUSED UNDERGROUND STATIONS

J E Connor

Capital Transport

Introduction

This book contains details of all Underground stations within the boundaries of the Greater London Boroughs closed between 1900 and 2006. Potted histories are supplied of each, but the length of these has been dictated by the amount of information available. Each station listed appears under the name it carried at time of closure.

The stations which I have included were all once the property of London Transport or its predecessors, and I have not featured any which belonged to main line companies. This category includes Uxbridge Road which was shared by West London Line services and LPTB trains until its demise in 1940.

Apart from total closures, where the station's name has been eradicated from the map, I have also included complete resitings. In addition, the more significant cases of street level buildings being resited have received a mention, but platforms which have been laterally relocated due to track-widening schemes, such as at Northwood and West Hampstead, have not.

There are also a few borderline cases, such as the original Farringdon Street terminus of 1863 and the old HCR premises at Hammersmith, where changes to alignment or siting indeed took place, but the movement was minimal.

Contents

KING WILLIAM STREET

Opened: 18.12.1890
Closed: 25.2.1900.

The first closed station we are dealing with had a life of just under ten years. It was the original northern terminus of the first electric tube railway in the world.

Having virtually completed work on the Tower Subway, the engineers Peter William Barlow and James Henry Greathead devised a similar, but more ambitious scheme to link Borough with King William Street in the City. They received Parliamentary authority for this, but there was little response from potential financiers, and the idea was set aside. It was revived in the following decade however, but this time the route was to stretch beyond Borough and terminate at Elephant & Castle instead.

The project became known as the City of London & Southwark Subway, and it received the Royal Assent on 28th July 1884, with Greathead appointed as Chief Engineer.

The CLSS was to comprise two separate running tunnels, and construction started in June 1886. To minimise disruption, staging was erected beside The Old Swan Pier near the north end of London Bridge, and an 82ft deep shaft was driven into the river bed. Four months later, on 28th October, the route for the northbound line began to be excavated, and the southbound tube followed in March of the following year.

With work well and truly under way, the directors felt that the route's potential would be improved if it was extended southwards to Stockwell. They therefore presented an additional Bill to Parliament, and received authorisation in 1887.

When completed, the company intended to operate single cars every two minutes, and employ cable haulage as its means of traction. This had been used on the London & Blackwall Railway in the 1840s, and although ingenious, and in many ways advanced for its time, it had to be abandoned after nine years, and replaced by locomotives. Nevertheless, by the 1880s, it seems that the technology involved had progressed considerably, and cable haulage was being used with success on certain tramways on the other side of the Atlantic. The CLSS was to employ Hallidie's patent cable system from America, but the patentees went into liquidation in 1888, and the company had to think again.

Steam traction had been ruled out by the authorising Act, so the directors decided to use electricity. Although still in its infancy at the time, this was proving successful overseas, and was ideally suited to a railway which would be completely in tunnel. Tenders were therefore invited, and the contract for providing the necessary electric equipment, including locomotives, was let to Mather & Platt of Salford in January 1889.

The following year, the CLSS was authorised to extend to Clapham, and the company name was changed to the City & South London Railway. This was sanctioned by an Act of 25th July 1890, and the directors felt that it was *more in harmony with the present nature and object of the undertaking.*

A general scene of 1897, which includes the street level building of King William Street station decorated for Queen Victoria's Diamond Jubilee in the background. The company name appears above the top floor, together with a sign recording its pioneering use of electric traction. Unfortunately, close-up views of the entrance, whilst still open, appear to be non-existent.

Entrance to the City terminus was provided from an existing building on the corner of King William Street and Arthur Street East (now Monument Street). One of the upper storeys accommodated the company offices, whilst the ground floor was adapted as a booking hall. From here a 25ft diameter liftshaft, provided with two hydraulic lifts, descended to a depth of 75ft, and provided passenger access to the trains, although in case of failures, there was also a flight of emergency stairs. There were two platforms, with one intended for departures, and the other arrivals, but the arrangement was rather odd, as these were situated either side of the same track. This was necessitated by the dictates of cable haulage, whereby a single car would arrive from the northbound line, and depart on the southbound without having to negotiate anything more complicated than a single set of points. Whilst the line was under construction, Stockwell was modified to accept two tracks, but similar work was not undertaken at the other end, and King William Street was therefore a bit of a curiosity, even from the outset.

The station approaches were also less than ideal, and were to prove very difficult to work. From the shaft at Old Swan Pier, the northbound tunnel was built immediately above the southbound, and had to dive down on either side so that they ran parallel. This involved the use of tortuous curves, and severe gradients, and although these may have suited cable traction, the arrangement was very taxing on the small four-wheeled electric locomotives subsequently employed. Old Swan Pier adjoined the north bank of the Thames, and lay to the west of London Bridge. Because of Parliamentary insistence that the line should not be constructed beneath buildings, unless specifically authorised to do so, the Company were obliged to pass beneath public thoroughfares. Therefore, from the river it followed Swan Lane, but as this was particularly narrow, the two tunnels were required to remain above each other, and could not level out until passing beneath Arthur Street West. Still following the road, the line then swung due east on a 140ft radius curve, and finally arrived at the terminus. The running tunnels on this section had an inside diameter of 10ft 2ins, and were lined with cast iron segments. At King William Street these emerged into a single 20ft high by 26ft wide bore, which had a 3ft lining of brick, and was finished in white glazed tiling. The premises were illuminated entirely by gas, and a signal box with nine levers was provided at the Stockwell end.

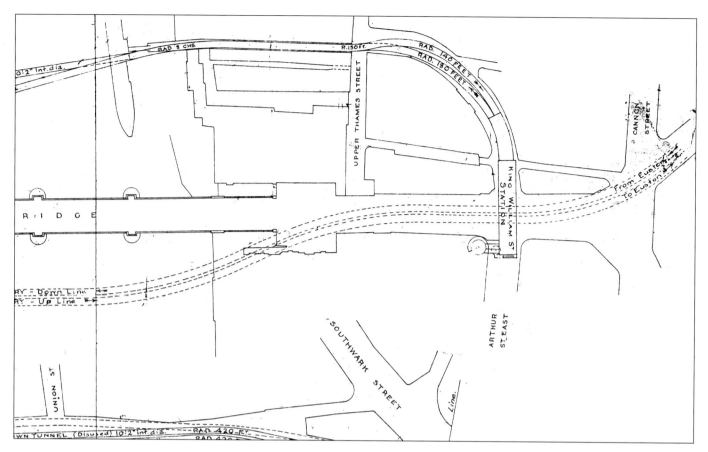

Map of King William Street
station end of the C&SLR.

Not only was the station badly laid out, the Company also had problems during its construction, as the water-logged ground adjoining the river gave way, and resulted in property damage around Arthur Street West and Cook's Lane. A number of houses and a coffee shop became subject to subsidence, and some received Dangerous Structure notices. The gas supply was also affected, and the walls of some buildings were so badly cracked that they required demolition.

On 13th November 1889, Major General C.S. Hutchinson RE inspected the running tunnels on behalf of the Board of Trade, and found that they had been built to the required standard.

The official opening of the line came on 4th November 1890, when HRH Edward, Prince of Wales (later King Edward VII), together with his son, the Duke of Clarence arrived at King William Street station and met various company officials. They then descended to the platforms, where they were greeted by the Lord Mayor and other civic dignitaries, before inspecting the inaugural train. This was hauled by locomotive No. 10 which had been specially painted in French grey and cream, and named

Princess of Wales Novr 4th 1890. The Prince was then given a golden key which carried the company's crest, and having performed the ceremony, boarded one of the two carriages which formed the special. This travelled to Oval, where the party alighted for a further inspection, then departed for Stockwell for a celebratory banquet. Afterwards, the guests returned to central London, but because of a major breakdown, they were obliged to forsake the railway and find other forms of transport instead.

Despite the earlier celebrations, various technical problems still had to be ironed out, and public traffic on London's first electric tube railway did not commence until 18th December 1890, when the inaugural train departed from Stockwell at 06.53.

Passengers using the line paid a standard fare of 2d, and passed through a turnstyle before entering the lift. At first tickets were not issued, but to avoid congestion at station entrances, returns were provided at a cost of 4d after 1892. These varied in style, but generally showed details of the journey above, and the issuing station below.

Within a year of opening, the layout at King William Street station was presenting serious operational problems, and at a company meeting in February 1892, the Chairman, Charles Grey Mott, described it as 'an engineering blunder'. A Bill was subsequently placed before Parliament to construct a new line from the Borough to Moorgate Street, and abandon the inadequate terminus completely.

This was authorised the following year, but in the meantime, traffic continued to grow, and something had to be done to alleviate problems at the City end, even if the station's days were by now numbered. There was no room for expansion in the existing building at No. 46 King William Street, so a lease was obtained on adjoining premises in Arthur Street East. These were modified to provide a Ladies Room, Parcels Room and Left Luggage Office. There was also a plan to install an additional lift, but the sinking of a new shaft would have been expensive, so the idea was duly dropped. By 1895, around 15,000 passengers were using King William Street each day, and delays resulting from the single platform road were causing chronic overcrowding. The company therefore decided to improve matters by replacing the platforms with a central island, and installing an extra track. The work on this was carried out with the minimum of traffic disruption, and was completed by December 1895. A scissors crossing was constructed at the Stockwell end, and this allowed arrivals and departures to use either line. Unfortunately this entailed platform shortening, so from then on, trains were restricted to three cars. The existing signal box was modified to suit the new arrangement, and had the number of its levers increased to twenty-two levers, of which five were spare.

Not all of the problems associated with King William Street could be dealt with so easily however, because the steep gradients and twisting tunnels proved an operational nightmare. On leaving the station, trains would head into the tube, then turn almost immediately towards the river, before descending at 1 in 30 to pass beneath the northbound tunnel near Swan Lane. Although initially running in the normal left handed manner, the crossing of tunnels resulted in them travelling on the right, and they did not revert to the left until after they got between Borough and Elephant & Castle. In the opposite direction, services approaching King William Street had to climb a 1 in 40 gradient to get over the other tunnel, and negotiate the 140ft radius Arthur Street

Curve almost immediately before arrival. This final stretch was subject to a severe Board of Trade speed restriction, although in reality the only way the little locomotives could hope to bring a fully loaded train into the terminus was to go as fast as possible on the descent beneath the river, and take a run at the opposing gradient. Sometimes they never succeeded, and the driver would allow his train to roll backwards, so he could make another attempt. If after a further try, the locomotive was still incapable, the engine at King William Street which was waiting to take the train back out, would be sent to the foot of the incline, couple up, and the pair would then double-head. As to what today's health and safety legislation would make of such practices is perhaps anybody's guess!

In an attempt to provide more seats on its services, the Company experimented with a 'motor-car' train, in which one of the vehicles was powered, and acted like a locomotive. By cutting out the space normally occupied by the little four-wheel engines, King William Street was capable of taking an extra vehicle, but time was lost as the driver fought his way from one end of the narrow crowded platform to the other whilst changing ends, and the scheme was soon dropped.

The contract for the extension to Moorgate Street was let to J. Mowlem & Company, and work commenced in the autumn of 1896. The new line diverged from the original at Borough Junction, a little to the north of Borough station, and took a far less tortuous route beneath the river than its predecessor. Tunnelling work

The former station building at King William Street, soon after the station closed, with a sign on the right offering the recently vacated accommodation for letting.

was hampered by having to underpin St Mary Woolnoth Church, where Bank station was to be constructed, but nevertheless by the end of 1898, all had been completed, and track laying could commence.

Once this had been done, the stations were made ready, and King William Street was officially closed from 25th February 1900. The extension to Moorgate Street was opened on the same date, and the 1,267 yards of earlier formation north of Borough Junction fell into disuse.

Apart from the largely experimental Tower Subway, this was the first stretch of underground railway in London to close, and *The Railway Magazine*, mindful of the wasted capital included this Pertinent Paragraph in its February 1901 edition: '*The present disused railway of the City & South London Railway under the Thames is apparently forgotten. How much unremunerative capital is sunk in it? Is it being maintained in proper condition, or is it simply being allowed to decay? Why not let it for mushroom culture, or bonded warehouses, or for some other dividend-providing purpose.*'

Two years before closure, a company called the City & Brixton Railway expressed a desire to purchase the tunnels, and incorporate them into a proposed new route, but this scheme failed to materialise. The track remained in position however, and was used for some years to store empty coaching stock. The abandonment of King William Street resulted in the CSLR offices being relocated to Moorgate Street, although delay in completion of the new accommodation meant that they had to remain at the disused station until the summer of 1900.

Obviously the idea of fungi cultivation caught on as the CSLR half-yearly meeting for 1910 was recorded in *The Railway Magazine*, and included this: '*As to the old tunnel from King William Street across the Thames, they* [the Company] *had received offers for it, one of which was that some adventurous growers of mushrooms wished to become tenants, but he thought they could do better with it than that, and perhaps they might let it to some telegraph or electric power company, who would find the old tube useful for carrying their cables ...*'

Unfortunately no such company was forthcoming, but with the advent of war in 1914, some thought the abandoned tunnels might play a more sinister role. Mr G.A. Nokes, the Editor of *The Railway & Travel Monthly*, suggested that a cell of enemy agents, complete with munitions and explosives may have been hiding in them, so a police search was organised. A careful inspection was made, and nothing was found, although in the interests of security the two tubes were subsequently boarded up at the Borough end, and a cover was placed above the old station lift-shaft.

Foreign spies or not, the disused formation continued to fascinate, and in response to two queries *The Railway Magazine* of February 1921 stated: '*The original tunnels from King William Street Station are still in existence, but the permanent way has been removed, and the ends, where they join the present lines, boarded up. They are not used for any specific purpose, except perhaps for storing p.w. material. Premises at street level are used as shops.*'

Nine years later the Underground Group decided to dispose of the former station by sale or lease, and invited a group of journalists along to provide publicity. One of those who took part in this visit was the historian Charles E. Lee, and he described the remains in *The Railway Magazine* of September 1930.

He noted that the platform surface had been removed, but otherwise a great deal survived, including the signal box, which still retained its twenty-two hand operated levers. Nearby, beside the commencement of the running tunnels, there were three two-aspect semaphore signals, and a faded board which stated '*Speed Not To Exceed 5 Miles Per Hour*'.

A great deal of tiling remained on the walls of the station tunnel, and in two places the name 'King William Street' could still be read, although the lettering which constituted this was far from complete.

No. 46 King William Street was eventually demolished in 1933, and its site taken by an office block named Regis House. The former station tunnel underneath remained untouched however, as did much of the original emergency stairs.

Soon after the Second World War started it was suggested that the abandoned sections south of the river would make an ideal air raid shelter, and the subject was discussed by a Council meeting of the Metropolitan Borough of Southwark in December 1939. The idea was subsequently approved by the Ministry of Home Security, and work started in January 1940.

To gain access to the former running tunnels, six new stairways were constructed, with an internal diameter of 9ft 9ins, and a lining of reinforced pre-cast concrete segments. Once again, the unstable nature of the surrounding

The platform tunnel around 1930, with part of the station name still visible on the tiling and the remains of a gas lamp on the left. Although the line was worked by electricity from the outset, it seems that gas was preferred as a means of station illumination.

The exit passages, again around 1930, showing the decorative bands of tiling which were employed on the early CSLR stations.

soil presented difficulties, but by tunnelling with compressed air, and the use of stabilising chemicals, these were overcome. When finished, concrete stairways were installed, and the entrances became capable of admitting three hundred people per minute.

Also in 1940, the owners of Regis House took out a tenancy on the old station tunnel, and converted it into a shelter with two floors. The majority of surviving relics must have disappeared at this time, although the emergency stairs were unaffected, as were the white tiled walls. An additional shaft was sunk from Arthur Street, and this provided access to another office block.

After the war, the six entrances into the former running tunnels were sealed off, and the formation returned to its slumber. At King William Street however, the converted station remained untouched and was used by the Regis House proprietors for document storage.

When visited by the author in the 1970s, it was like stepping into a time warp. Much of the shelter accommodation remained untouched, and slightly faded, but otherwise perfect wartime propaganda posters stared down from the walls. Amongst these were some of the 'Careless Talk Costs Lives' classics by the artist Cyril Kenneth Bird, better known as 'Fougasse', which emphasised the importance of secrecy with cartoons of unsuspecting people having conversations overheard by Hitler. It was a particularly hot day, but down below, the former running tunnels were dank and cold, with stalactites hanging from the cast-iron segments.

Regis House was demolished at the beginning of 1995, and subsequently replaced by a new building of the same name, whilst down below, the City terminus of the world's first electric tube railway continues to survive, albeit drastically converted as an air raid shelter in 1940.

Above left The platform surface was removed after closure, leaving just its supports. When visited by journalists in 1930, it was noted that the signal box still contained its twenty-two hand operated levers.

Below left A section of running tunnel on the approach to the station.

Above The former station tunnel adapted as an air-raid shelter in 1940. The posters add a bit of cheer to an otherwise gloomy scene.

Left Amazingly, some of the posters survived into the 1970s, including some of the famous 'Careless Talk Costs Lives' designs by 'Fougasse'.

When the former station tunnel at King William Street was converted into an air raid shelter in 1940, an additional floor was installed to increase accommodation. This resulted in a number of earlier features being lost, but some of the old ceramic tiling survived and is clearly seen in the photograph reproduced here.

The tiling scheme used on City & South London Railway stations was overall white, with waistbands in dark chocolate brown. King William Street's platform level decorative courses largely disappeared during the changes of 1940, but the odd section remained untouched.

Opposite The stairway at King William Street retained its decorative courses and provides a good example of early City & South London Railway tiling.

'NORTH END'

Partially constructed by CCEHR,
but never opened.
Now generally referred to as 'Bull & Bush'.

When the Charing Cross, Euston & Hampstead Railway was planned, the company intended to build a station known as North End, between Golders Green and Hampstead.

The authorising Act of 1903 included powers to acquire two and a half acres of land around and including Wyldes Farmhouse for its construction, and work began at track level.

However, in the summer of 1903, the Hampstead Heath Extension Council, inspired by the veteran philanthropist Mrs Henrietta Barnett, contacted the LCC with a view to purchasing 80 acres of land north of the station site, and retaining them as a permanent open space. At this time, a scheme was well advanced to develop the area, but because of opposition this failed to materialise, and in September 1904 the plot was sold to the conservationists.

Mrs Barnett had no objection to the station being constructed, and in fact thought it was a good idea, as it would provide a convenient means of access to the Heath for people who wished to travel there from other parts of London. However, the lack of local housing was thought to offer a bleak future for North End, and the CCEHR began to doubt whether it was going to be worth the investment.

Nevertheless, work on the platforms, cross passages and lower stairs had been started, and three lifts were ordered from Otis Electric in March 1906. The wisdom of this extravagance was soon doubted however, as a few weeks later the Works Committee decided that if only two lifts were employed, it would only prove necessary to construct a single liftshaft, and therefore cut down on costs. In fact, neither this nor the shaft for emergency stairs was ever driven, because soon afterwards the Company decided to forget the whole business and the station remained unfinished.

The street level building would have stood on the north side of Hampstead Way and opposite Wyldes Farmhouse, but this was never constructed, and the site was sold for residential use in 1927. Since abandonment, the intended name has been largely forgotten, as it is generally referred to by staff as 'Bull &

Bush'. However, this is rather misleading, as the hostelry of that name, immortalised in song by the music hall singer Florrie Forde is located about a quarter of a mile away.

Having always been cut off from the outside world, access from the surface was finally provided in the 1950s, when a spiral staircase was installed to serve a floodgate control room, which had been built at low level, and connected to the aborted station workings below. In addition a small manual lift was constructed, although its upper landing stopped short of the surface, so those using it had to continue by way of the stairs up to the exit, a thick concrete structure.

This access was to prove useful in 1978, when current health and safety requirements led to the removal of 430yds of asbestos lining, which had been installed in the southbound tunnel between Golders Green and Hampstead forty-six years earlier. Before this could take place, both ends of the section had to be blocked by double doors, and a restricted peak-hour service introduced, which worked in both directions on the northbound line. A gang of around forty men then set about removing the asbestos, and packing it into polythene bags. These were then gathered on the site where the northbound platform would have been, and collected by special engineers' trains which ran when the line was not in public use.

The site of North End station is marked by gaps beside the track, and these can be seen from a passing train. It is understood that the platforms were indeed constructed, or at least part-constructed; these have since been removed. Sections remain within the cross-passages however, although whether these were surfaced before the project was abandoned is not certain. The segments which form the station tunnels were in-filled, presumably to provide a base for the wall tiles, but these were never added. The lower stairways were more or less completed, although it is thought that the stair treads were never fitted and, as with the platform area, no tiling was carried out.

Although the station was never opened, much of the fabric below ground still survives. The top of the access shaft is covered by a squat concrete structure surrounded by palisade fencing, located on the western side of Hampstead Way. At low level, the staircase and passageway shafts have been constructed but no evidence exists for any finishes ever having been applied. Access to the platforms is not possible but the space they would have occupied is clearly observable while travelling through by train.

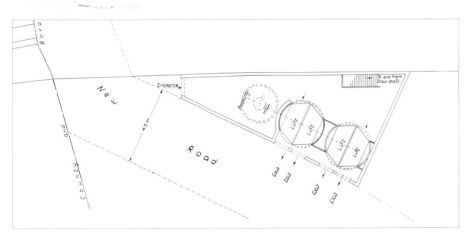

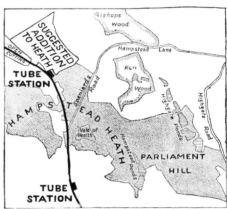

A map published in 1904 showing the locations of two stations on the new tube line which were intended to serve the area. That at the bottom is Hampstead, or Heath Street as it was known prior to opening, whilst above is North End, adjoining the land proposed for the Heath extension.

Centre This ground plan, like the drawing above, dates from about 1902 when the station at North End was being planned. It shows the building with exits on to a new road on the west side of the station. The artist's impression of how the station may have looked was produced specially for this book as no contemporary perspectives or elevations exist. It shows the side looking on to Hampstead Way. The exits would have been at the back and facing a planned new road.

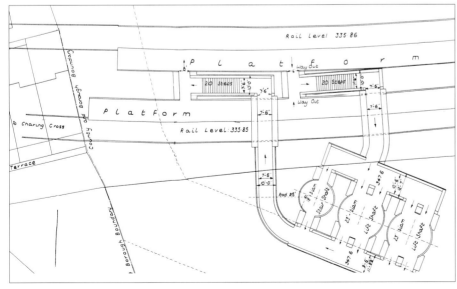

Left Plan of the intended layout of North End platforms and lift shafts.

Although no work was carried out above ground, the station tunnels at North End were constructed, complete with cross passages and partly finished stairways. A writer in the Railway Observer for July 1954 recalled that "the platform edges were cut back about 1933" with the presumed object of reducing maintenance." These views show the southbound side and look towards Golders Green.

Two views of unfinished stairways at North End.

One of the original North End station subways now joins up with the bottom of the new lift shaft up a short flight of steps. If you go through the door and turn left you come to the steps shown on the upper picture on page 21. You turn right to enter the floodgate control room.

Steps up to 1950s lift from original North End station subway (you can see two diamond shapes at the top of the steps. This is the bottom of the steps so the surface on the 1950s lower lift landing. The lift is opposite.

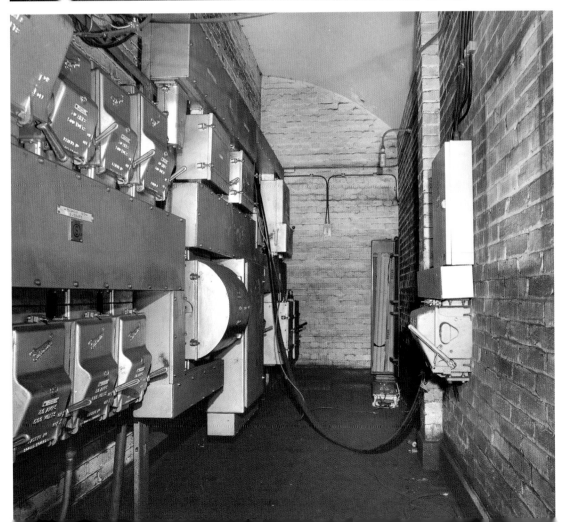

Switch room at south end of southbound platform area

HOUNSLOW TOWN

Opened as Hounslow: 1.5.1883
Renamed Hounslow Town: 1884
Temporarily Closed: 1.4.1886–1.3.1903
Closed: 2.5.1909

On 26th August 1880, the Hounslow & Metropolitan Railway was authorised to construct a 5½ mile line from Mill Hill Park (now Acton Town) on the Metropolitan District Railway to a terminus opposite Hounslow Barracks. At this time, the MDR was keen to expand its suburban system, and in November of the following year deposited a Bill to construct an additional 2½ miles of track which would connect this branch with the London & South Western Railway between Twickenham and Strawberry Hill. Unfortunately, the LSWR regarded this scheme as an aggressive intrusion into its territory, and after fierce opposition succeeded in it being abandoned.

Work continued on the remainder of the route however, and although Parliamentary authority was not forthcoming for the connecting line, the Company began constructing this in 1882. It commenced at a spot known as Lampton Junction, and despite original hopes, it was destined to remain a branch for the rest of its days. It stretched for a distance of 2f 5ch and terminated abruptly above Hounslow High Street, where a bridge would have been built if the earlier scheme had become a reality. Like the rest of the route from Mill Hill Park it was double track throughout, although the 1m 44ch section between Lampton Junction and Hounslow Barracks was to be completed as a single line.

Whilst making his Board of Trade inspection in April 1883, Colonel Yolland noted that a short section of line continued beyond the limits of deviation at Hounslow Town, and although this had been constructed purely by consent of local landowners, a Bill was before Parliament to legalise it. At this time, it was deemed acceptable to construct a railway without official sanction on land which had been acquired by voluntary agreement, providing it did not cross a public road, or infringe on tidal waters. Colonel Yolland found that the standard of construction was satisfactory, and approved the line from Hounslow to Mill Hill Park as being suitable for public use. Trains commenced running a week or so later on 1st May, although

Parliamentary authority for the branch section was not actually received until 29th June. The terminus was opened as 'Hounslow', but was renamed Hounslow Town during the following year. It comprised two platforms, and was controlled by a signal box containing twenty levers, of which four were spare at time of opening.

On 21st July 1884, the single track section from Lampton Junction to Hounslow Barracks was brought into use, and the branch serving the Town became a superfluous appendage. Within a short while, the MDR decided that this was no longer worth retaining, so a replacement station named Heston–Hounslow was constructed on the new line, and the earlier terminus closed from 1st April 1886.

In May 1901, *The Railway Magazine* included the following description of the abandoned branch under its Pertinent Paragraphs heading: '*The derelict line to the Hounslow Town Station is about half a mile in length, and was constructed in the most substantial manner with a double set of rails, about one-half of it being on a brick viaduct of twenty arches. There is (or was) an imposing station, a signal-box, engine line with coal stage, engine pit, water tank and column, a complete system of signals, with interlocking, and, in fact, everything required on a first-class line of railway. But time has wrought havoc with the disused line, the flooring of the two platforms is gone (except under the covered portion), and the beams are fast decaying. Only one connection (the down) remains with the used portion of the railway, the points, and a short length of up line, it is true, are still in situ at the junction, but the remainder of the rails up to the up platform have been taken up, as also have the crossings and rails at the "dead end" of the platforms. The station-house buildings are occupied as a dwelling-house, and the covered portion of the platform is used for hanging out the family washing, while a solitary cock fowl is to be seen strutting about on the platform, and is apparently "monarch of all he surveys." At any rate, we did not stay "to dispute his rights."*

'The station yard and some of the arches are let to the District Council for storing steam rollers, dust carts, and other articles for which the Council's offices are not adequately adapted.

'The station abuts on the High Street, Hounslow, and is a good position for obtaining traffic, whilst the newer station; Heston-Hounslow – some three-quarters of a mile away is some distance off the high road, and is, therefore, at a disadvantage in this respect. The Metropolitan District Railway is always ready to extend, and therefore if a line to the neighbourhood of Hampton Court were proposed no doubt this derelict line would be the commencement of it.'

No such line was ever constructed, but despite the apparently poor condition of the terminus, the branch was still not dead. On 1st March 1903, the derelict station was re-opened, and provided with two trains an hour throughout the day, with more in the peak periods. Soon after, on 21st July 1903, the Hounslow & Metropolitan Railway was bought by the MDR for around £166,000, and an electrification scheme for it was announced.

As part of the associated improvements, a new 7.42ch western curve was constructed to link the branch with the Hounslow Barracks line at what became known as Kingsley Road Junction. This consisted of a single track, and had a ruling gradient of 1 in 106. The radius varied from 3 to 4 chains, and being so sharp, it had to be fitted with a check rail throughout. Because of this curvature, the line was subject to an 8mph speed restriction, and it was not deemed suitable for steam locomotives. It was brought into use with the introduction of electric services on 13th June 1905, and used by all Hounslow line services. These ran via Hounslow Town terminus, where they reversed, and for a while there were no public workings on the direct route between Lampton Junction and Kingsley Road Junction. Immediately prior to electrification, down trains, formed of eight coaches, would divide at Osterley, with five vehicles continuing to Hounslow Barracks, and the remaining three to Hounslow Town. A similar arrangement was worked in the opposite direction, with the two portions joining at Osterley, and proceeding to either Mill Hill Park or Mansion House as a single train.

The service frequency was improved from the beginning of January 1909, when two-car electric trains commenced working every ten minutes between Mill Hill Park and Hounslow Barracks, via Hounslow Town. At the reopened terminus, the signal box had been

brought back into full use, and equipped with four circuit section indicators. In his Board of Trade inspection report dated 10th June 1905, Colonel J.W. Pringle noted: 'At Hounslow Town the signal box is old and the existing mechanical frame has been re-locked in accordance with the new Hounslow Curve. The interlocking is correct. An old crossover road at the platforms has to be pulled out.' He also mentioned that no alterations had been made to any of the stations along the route, and does not make reference to repairs having been carried out at the terminus. This is perhaps surprising, considering the description given in the May 1901 *Railway Magazine*, which implied that the platforms had been partially demolished, and the premises were in a pretty bad shape.

In its early days, traffic levels on the line towards Hounslow Barracks were never particularly encouraging, but following electrification things began to improve. To speed up operations, the MDR decided to build a new Hounslow Town station on the through line, and close the original. This took place on 2nd May 1909, and the old terminus fell into disuse for the final time. It was later completely demolished, and the site redeveloped as a London General Omnibus Company garage, which functioned from 14th July 1912 until 1954 when it was replaced by new premises to the north.

Today, passengers can still glimpse the site of Lampton Junction from a passing train, but the little terminus at the corner of Hounslow High Street and Kingsley Road has disappeared without trace.

Unfortunately photographs of the station appear to be particularly rare, but this is perhaps understandable after reading from the following which was included in the Company's Sectional Appendix of May 1901, and referred to the entire MDR system:
'An instance having come under notice of attempts being made to take Photographs upon the Line and Stations by outsiders, Station Inspectors and all concerned, are hereby instructed to be specially on the alert to prevent anything of this kind being done without authority. Anyone observed on the premises proceeding to arrange to take photographs, sketches or measurements must be required to produce a WRITTEN authority before being allowed to do so.'

CITY ROAD

Opened: 17.11.1901
Closed: 9.8.1922

The station was opened by the City & South London Railway on 17th November 1901 with the route from Moorgate Street to Angel, and had its surface building at the junction of City Road and Moreland Street. This contained the booking office and a men's toilet, although unlike the other pair of stations on the same extension, there were no similar facilities for women. Emergency stairs were installed, but the main passenger access to the platforms was afforded by a pair of Easton Anderson electric lifts. These were each capable of accommodating fifty-five people, and were contained within a single shaft with a depth of 65ft.

Down below, there were two platforms, and a signal box, which when inspected by the Board of Trade around the time of opening contained eight levers, of which three were spare.

From the very outset City Road appears to have been little used, and after just a few years it seemed that closure would be likely. The subject was brought up at a Board meeting on 30th June 1908, and it was recorded that '*The Solicitor was of the opinion that the Company are not under any legal obligation to keep the station open.*'

Nevertheless, trains continued to call, although there was clearly no real demand.

The street level building of City Road station, as it appeared prior to closure. The entrance can be seen to the far right, whilst the exit, leading directly from the lifts, adjoins the tobacconist's shop, and is topped by a lamp.

It was only 48 chains from Old Street, and 25 chains from Angel, and even then the surrounding area was rather run down. City Road itself however has long been well known, and its Eagle Tavern was once a popular venue for Londoners. Attached to this was a place of entertainment known as The Grecian Hall, and here at the tender age of 15, little Matilda Wood, better known by her professional name of Marie Lloyd gave her first public performance in 1886.

Unlike 'Our Marie' however, City Road station led a particularly humdrum and unsuccessful career. On 26th August 1916, it witnessed an unfortunate accident, when a guard started a train whilst a passenger was alighting, and the unfortunate man was dragged to his death.

Control of the CSLR had passed to the Underground Electric Railways of London group on 1st January 1913, but no significant changes took place until after the First World War. Automatic signalling began to be introduced from 1919, and around the same time, experiments in widening the diameter of the tunnels were taking place at its southern end.

As built, the tubes on the section of line on which City Road was situated had a diameter of 10ft 6ins. This restricted the type of stock that was operated, and as the former CSLR was to be incorporated into what we now know as the Northern Line, something had to be done. Therefore after receiving government agreement on funding, the work commenced in 1922.

The standard diameter of the new running tunnels was 11ft 8¼ins, and although an attempt was made to enlarge the bores with minimum disruption to traffic, it was found to be easier if services were suspended. Therefore from 9th August 1922, trains were temporarily withdrawn from the section north of Moorgate Street, and passengers were transferred to a replacement service operated by the London General Omnibus Company, which was also part of the Underground Group.

The line reopened on 20th April 1924, but City Road was destined to remain closed. A ventilation shaft was subsequently installed incorporating the passageway leading to the old northbound side, but other than this the only activity was the removal of its platforms.

During the Second World War however, City Road was earmarked for conversion into an air raid shelter, although work on this did not start until the worst of the Blitz was actually over. In June 1941, Mr Ove Arup set out a plan whereby the former station tunnels could be converted to include a second floor, and therefore making them capable of holding four hundred and ninety-nine shelterers.

Although a similar scheme proved acceptable at British Museum, it was rejected at City Road, and therefore the conversion got the go ahead on the understanding that it provided accommodation at track level only. After this, work started on the construction of a six-foot high brick wall, which was built to provide a screen between the shelter and passing trains. The top of this would be left open to improve ventilation, but in the interest of safety, a covering of wire mesh would be used.

Before this could be added however, it was decided to go ahead with the two-level scheme, and 6in pre-cast flooring units were delivered to Golders Green depot by Truscon Floors in August 1941. Work was well advanced by the final months of that year, and the cost of completion, including ventilation, was anticipated to be around £1,855.

Public access to the premises was by way of the former street level building, but a new stairway had to be constructed to link with the original passageways down below. Part of the passage leading to the old southbound platform was adapted to provide toilet facilities, but the other was unavailable as it was part of the ventilation system.

When built, the station's two platforms had been linked by five cross passages, and these were each equipped with wooden stairs to allow access between the two shelter levels. According to drawings produced by the Regional Headquarters of the London Civil Defence, there was a short section of platform at the Angel end of the southbound side to aid deliveries to an adjoining canteen, but as it is understood that the original platforms had gone by this time, it seems likely that this was a temporary wooden staging. All the facilities were situated at this end, with a canteen on the southbound, and a medical aid post on the northbound.

Following the return to peace, the shelter was dismantled, and the grimy white tiled platform walls were again visible from a passing train. Up above, the street level building, topped by an incongruous ventilation tower survived intact until the 1960s, or possibly 1970s, when the majority of it was demolished. A fragment survived until recently at the base of the tower however, and the site of the platforms can still be seen by the observant passenger.

The former street level building at City Road, as it appeared in the late 1960s.

Although the platforms at City Road have long since disappeared, the station site remains clearly visible from passing trains.

The street level building has been used for various commercial purposes since closure and this view shows it in 2021.

The platforms were removed many years ago, but their former locations remain visible from passing trains. Much of the tiling has been obliterated beneath a thick layer of paint, but the dark red 'rings' above the tracks have not been similarly treated.

The lifts at South Kentish Town were removed many years ago and the shafts were plugged, but this side of the lower lift landing retained many of its original features.

This is the footbridge above the northbound line at South Kentish Town which led from the lower lift landing to the platform stairs.

The south side of the lower lift landing at South Kentish Town.

One of the two stairways at South Kentish Town which linked the lower lift landings with the platforms.

The site of the northbound platform at South Kentish Town, with the footbridge which once served the exit stairs in the upper foreground.

The passageway at the base of the stairs which led down from the booking hall at South Kentish Town.

Far left The base of the stairs which led down from booking hall.

Left The upper section of the booking hall stairs with their walls clad to waist height in green tiling. This was one of the many features at South Kentish Town which were typical of the stations designed by the architect, Leslie W. Green.

PARK ROYAL & TWYFORD ABBEY

Opened: 23.6.1903
Resited: 6.7.1931

This station was opened on the Ealing & South Harrow Railway on 23rd June 1903 and had its entrance on the south side of Twyford Abbey Road. It consisted of two wooden platforms, a footbridge and some fairly basic buildings. Immediately to the east lay the 102 acre Royal Agricultural Showground from which the station took its name, but there was little nearby habitation and the immediate surroundings were still rural.

At first it was used as a temporary terminus for Metropolitan District Railway electric trains from Mill Hill Park (now Acton Town), because the earthworks towards South Harrow had been damaged by a sustained bout of heavy rain, and were not deemed safe enough for use. Its opening was timed to coincide with that of the Royal Agricultural Show in the adjoining grounds, but the attendance was poor, and the initial public response to the station was therefore disappointing.

The problems with the formation were soon rectified, and trains began to run the full length of the line five days later.

Although officially named 'Park Royal & Twyford Abbey', and shown as such on the nameboards, the suffix does not seem to have been included on MDR tickets.

With the spread of suburbia in the inter-war years, the station, in common with many others of its type, was proving inadequate for the growing population. In most cases rebuilds were carried out on existing sites, but in this case completely new premises were preferred. The district around nearby Western Avenue was fast developing into a thriving neighbourhood of houses and factories, so this was thought to be a much better location.

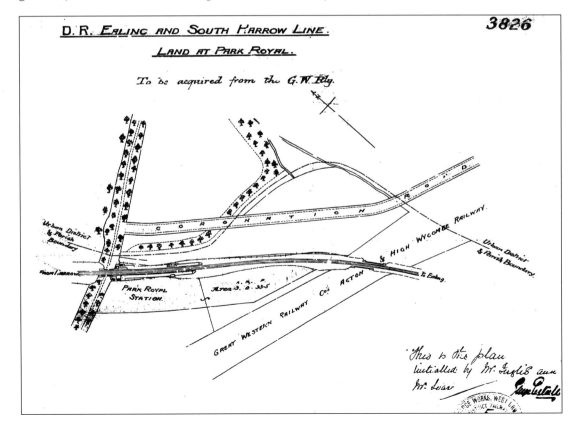

The replacement platforms were sited about 30ch east of their predecessors, and stretched to a length of 425ft. They were brought into use on 6th July 1931, when the original station was closed, although the constructional work was still unfinished, and the accompanying buildings were of a temporary nature.

The new station, named 'Park Royal', was reached by means of a temporary booking office at street level on the up side, which had previously been used during the rebuilding of Ealing Common. Beyond lay a footbridge, also transported from Ealing Common, and this in turn led to the two platforms. These were formed of pre-cast concrete slabs, and were surfaced with ash. The up side was provided with a 10ft x 8ft wooden shelter, close to the stairs from street level, and electric lighting was installed from the outset.

The Great Western Railway constructed a pathway to the new station from their halt at Park Royal West, which opened in June 1932, but even at the time, the inspecting officer, Col. A.H.L. Mount, stated he *'gathered that it was doubtful whether the small interchange of traffic is likely to justify this connecting link.'*

The permanent street level building of the new Park Royal station was erected on the opposite side of the line from the temporary entrance, and was completed in March 1936. It was designed by Felix Lander, and featured a distinctive 67ft tower, with illuminated LPTB roundels on each of its faces. One side of this adjoined a circular booking hall, with a diameter of 40ft, whilst another led into a curved parade of shops. It is a particularly fine piece of 1930s London Transport architecture, and since January 1987 has been a listed structure.

The old station at Park Royal & Twyford Abbey was of course far less substantial in its construction, and following closure it was soon demolished.

The entrance to the first Park Royal station, with stairs leading from the un-surfaced Twyford Abbey road to the platform-level booking office. At the time of opening, the surroundings were still decidedly rural, and rather frugal corrugated-iron buildings were deemed sufficient for the envisaged traffic.

DOWN STREET

Opened: 15.3.1907
Closed: 22.5.1932

The station at Down Street, situated between Dover Street (now Green Park) and Hyde Park Corner on the Great Northern Piccadilly & Brompton Railway, seemed to have had problems from the outset.

On 20th October 1903, when the line was still at its planning stage, the engineer responsible for this section, Sir James W. Szlumper, submitted a set of plans for the station to the Board of Trade, but it seems that the subterranean passageways were too long and intricate. It was felt that these could exacerbate problems in the event of an emergency, but as there was seemingly no realistic alternative to Szlumper's layout, it was cautiously approved four days later.

Unfortunately, the problems did not end there however, as Szlumper again wrote to the Board of Trade on 27th October stating that there was difficulty in acquiring a site for the street level building, so the scheme would have to be completely revised.

This was achieved, but a year later the BoT was apparently still worried about possible dangers, as an internal memo of 20th October 1904 stated: '*The plan is open to the objections that the entrance to the stairway from the platforms is situated a long way from the lifts. If therefore the lifts were not available passengers seeking to escape would have to retrace their steps from the lifts in order to reach the stairway. To attempt to do this in time of panic or in a crush would be hopeless. The plan should be modified so that a direct access to the stairway shall be available to passengers who might find the lifts closed or out of use. There should be no need for passengers to turn back.*'

Szlumper submitted an amended drawing on 4th November, and at long last this met with full approval.

These difficulties no doubt had a bearing on the station's being one of three which were not ready for opening with the Finsbury Park to Hammersmith route on 15th December 1906. Nevertheless work on it continued, and it was eventually brought into use on 15th March 1907.

The surface building, designed by Leslie W. Green, was located on the south-west side of Down Street, and was connected to the platforms by means of a single liftshaft. This had a depth of 60.68ft, and accommodated a pair of Otis Electric lifts. There were also the customary emergency stairs, which in common with the station tunnels and passageways were tiled in maroon and cream.

It seems that the Company may not have been particularly satisfied with the station's name, as 'G.A. Sekon' writing in *The Railway Magazine* of February 1907 stated that it was '*to be re-christened Mayfair*'. This never happened however, although the bullseye nameboards which were carried in later years included 'Mayfair' as a suffix.

Unfortunately, Down Street failed to attract much custom. It was less than 550yds from Hyde Park Corner, and just over 600yds from Dover Street, and there was little demand for it from the immediate locality. It was tucked away, off the main thoroughfare of Piccadilly, in a district where people had access to private transport or else used cabs. Not surprisingly, it was one of the stations missed by certain trains after 1909, and it lost its Sunday services from 5th May 1918.

An internal report dated September 1929 listed ten stations on the Piccadilly Line with a view to the closure of some stations to speed up the journey time following the opening of extensions to the north and west of London. Based on sample surveys, the passenger takings and annual usage figures were as follows:

Aldwych	£4500	1,069,650
Down Street	£5005	1,236,250
Brompton Street	£5180	971,350
York Road	£5243	1,208,700
Regents Park	£5391	1,208,150
Mornington Crescent	£5994	1,190,550
Hyde Park Corner	£8050	1,847,550
Gillespie Road	£8675	2,548,750
Gloucester Road	£9262	1,741,900
Covent Garden	£10,028	2,502,350

The exterior of Down Street station in its early days. The platforms were both 350ft long, and were positioned next to each other in parallel tubes. Today, the bricked off platforms can just be made out from passing trains.

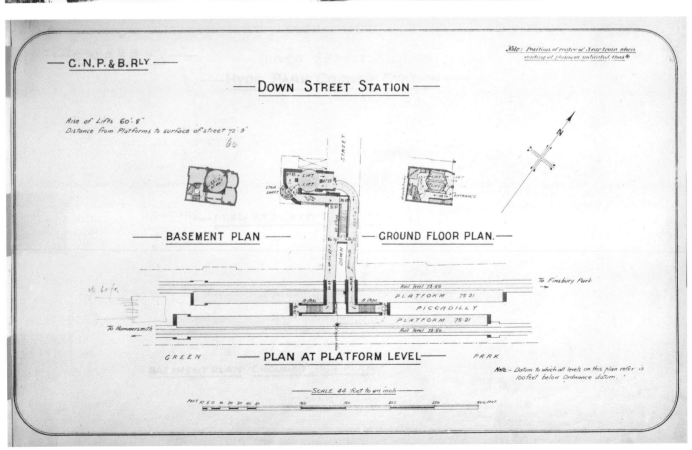

CLOSING OF EXISTING STATIONS:

With this same object of raising the average speed to 25 m.p.h., consideration should be given to closing the following stations at the time the new Line is opened:-

Park Royal. (Extension of bus services from Park Royal to N. Ealing to be considered.)
Gloucester Road. (P.& B.)
Brompton Road.
Down Street. (Bus stops to be instituted)
Covent Garden.
York Road.
Caledonian Road.
Gillespie Road. (To be opened specially for football matches, etc. numbering about 40 occasions per year.)

The closing of Barons Court, on the District side, should also be investigated.

Computer generated view of Down Street platform bullseye sign with Mayfair suffix.

Down Street station shortly before closure

On 4th June 1930, the Royal Assent was given to extend the Piccadilly Line from Finsbury Park to Cockfosters, and also to install a siding between Down Street and Hyde Park Corner. The latter required partial demolition of the platforms at Down Street, but by now the station was in its final days, and closure was inevitable. The last train departed on 21st May 1932, and work on the new siding could then start in earnest.

This was located between the eastbound and westbound lines, and stretched for a length of about 836ft. It was accommodated within a new tube of 14ft 6in diameter, and had its track offset slightly to one side to allow space for a walkway. The siding was chiefly intended for reversing trains, as traffic on the eastern end of the Piccadilly was noticeably heavier than that on the western, but it was also equipped with servicing facilities. These included an inspection pit, which continued from end to end, and the generous diameter of the tunnel allowed a disabled car to be lifted off its bogies. The track was laid on a 20ch curve, and was long enough to take two seven-car trains. It was controlled from the existing signal box at Hyde Park Corner, although the twelve-lever Westinghouse frame needed to be completely reconditioned, and provided with eleven more levers. Staff access to the siding was by means of a 7ft diameter passageway, which connected its western end with the east end of Hyde Park Corner station.

To allow room for the necessary pointwork, the western extremities of the now-disused platforms at Down Street had to be removed, and their site levelled. When the new siding was being inspected on behalf of the Ministry of Transport on 29th May 1933, the inspecting officer, Lt. Col. E. Woodhouse, noted that a door leading to a relay room and store located in one of the old cross-passages, now opened directly onto the positive rail instead of the eastbound platform as before. This was clearly a source of danger, but the Company agreed to keep the door permanently closed, and the siding was brought into use the following day.

For the remainder of the decade, Down Street station slumbered in its dark tunnel, but as the clouds of war began to gather over Europe, a completely new use was found for it.

The various underground passageways were fitted out as offices, and became the headquarters of the Railway Executive Committee. Being in such a convenient part of the West End, it was also used by the War Cabinet, and Winston Churchill was reputedly often seen walking across Green Park en-route between Whitehall and Down Street.

As the street level building had been leased to Angel Botibol, the tobacconists, access was made available through a doorway at the Piccadilly end of the frontage. This led onto a concrete-lined stairway, and eventually the former emergency stairs. By this time, the lift-shaft had been adapted to provide extra tunnel ventilation, and the original lifts had long gone. A small cigar-shaped lift was fitted for wartime use however, although this was very cramped, and could only accommodate about two people at a time.

At track level, the cream and maroon tile-work was largely obliterated by matt grey paint, and walls were erected to screen activity from passing trains. Behind these was more office accommodation, and a fully equipped telephone exchange, but of course, all this was unbeknown to the general public. A fragment of platform was retained on either side, and would be used as necessary for setting down or picking up those who had business there. So that drivers knew when to stop for the latter, a plunger-operated red light was fitted in both tunnels, and anyone boarding the train had to do so by way of the leading cab.

When the war ended, Down Street reverted to complete disuse, although many of the wartime fittings, including toilets and two bathrooms remained in position. These con-

tinue to survive at the time of writing, as does the emergency stairwell, although the actual stairs have been replaced in recent years. Visible cream and maroon tiling is now confined to the stairways and passages, as that at platform level continues to be largely obliterated by grey paint. Some of the fired-on directional signs survive, together with fragments of name panels, but, because the site is bricked-off from the running lines, very little can be seen from a passing train.

Down Street with later added canopy, seen in 1924.

A section of the emergency stairs at Down Street, together with a small lift added for use during the Second World War.

The curving passageway which connected the lower lift landing at Down Street with the platform stairs.

Looking towards the lower lift landing from the 'entrance' subway.

One of the two flights of stairs at Down Street linking the platforms with the lower lift landing.

The lift shaft in 2009 with the entrance subway on the far side. A new walkway has been provided across the lift shaft above the lift well for emergency egress.

When the station was being altered to serve its wartime role, much of the platform tiling was painted over. However, some sections remained visible, including that adjoining a headwall on the westbound side, which features this nice "No Exit" cartouche.

Looking up the alternative emergency stairs which have been partitioned to create more rooms.

The passageway which linked the lower lift landing with the platform stairways, looking back towards the emergency stairs.

YORK ROAD

Opened: 15.12.1906
Closed: 19.9.1932

Opened by the Great Northern Piccadilly & Brompton Railway on 15th December 1906, York Road was situated between the stations at King's Cross and Caledonian Road.

The street level building was sited at the corner of York Road (now York Way) and Bingfield Street, and was designed by the architect Leslie William Green. It was built by the firm of Ford & Walton Ltd at a cost of £8,176 and was clad in £1,022.5.9d's worth of glazed ruby-red tiling by the Leeds Fireclay Company.

The booking hall was linked to the platforms by way of emergency stairs and a single 23ft diameter liftshaft. This contained two electric lifts supplied by the Otis Elevator Company, and these were recorded as having a rise of 89.49ft when inspected by Colonel H.A. Yorke on behalf of the Board of Trade around the time of opening. At York Road, the lifts descended directly to platform level, whereas those at the majority of other GNPBR stations required passengers to alight at a lower landing, then walk down a flight of stairs before reaching the trains. Although unusual, this arrangement was not unique to York Road, as it was also a feature at Caledonian Road, King's Cross and Earl's Court. It made little difference to the general layout however, although the cross-passages were wider as a result.

The westbound platform had a length of 351ft 9ins, whilst the eastbound was fractionally shorter at 350ft. Both were constructed from concrete and each had a width of 10ft. The parallel station tunnels had a diameter of 21ft 2½ins, and were tiled by the firm of George Wooliscroft & Son from Hanley in Staffordshire. The background colour of the tiling was white, whilst the patterning, typical of Leslie Green's stations, was picked out in two shades of red. Ventilation was by means of a fan, which was capable of exhausting 18,500 cu.ft. of air per minute.

There was a crossover immediately to the north-east of the station, and to operate this a signal cabin containing a small locking frame was provided at the Finsbury Park end of the eastbound platform.

The station was located in a fairly poor district, and failed to attract a great deal of custom. Even at the outset there seemed to be doubts about its prospects, as 'G.A. Sekon' wrote in *The Railway Magazine* of February 1907: '*The company has also provided railway facilities for another portion of Islington – hitherto without railway accommodation – the district west of Caledonian Road, the York Road station serving it. Much interest attaches to the experiment of planting railway stations in these districts, but time will prove whether the inhabitants of the parts thus favoured rise to the occasion by liberally patronising the Great Northern, Piccadilly and Brompton Railway.*'

From October 1909, some trains ceased to call in a bid to accelerate services, and Sunday trains were withdrawn completely from 5th May 1918. With the onset of the General Strike it closed on 4th May 1926, and may well have fallen into permanent disuse. However as this would have been a source of local inconvenience, the subject was raised in the House of Commons, and York Road reopened on 4th October of the same year. As part of a scheme to increase line capacity, it was closed for the second time on 19th September 1932, but this time it was to prove permanent. A few months later, an oversight on behalf of the operating department resulted in this little quip appearing in the February 1933 edition of the staff magazine '*T.O.T*': '*A bit late to mention Christmas, but we went to press just before the Traffic Circular appeared with the news that York Road would be closed for Christmas Day. We were strongly in favour of this, and can only hope that the staff enjoyed this extension of their holiday which has lasted since September 17th.*' As there was no Sunday service, trains ceased to call after traffic on Saturday 17th, but as is customary in these matters, the official date of closure was the following Monday.

The platforms were subsequently removed, but until the 1960s, it was still possible to clearly see the grimy tiling from a passing train. A new crossover was installed at King's Cross on 25th November 1956, and practically

Leslie W. Green's street level building at York Road, seen soon after opening.

Above The eastbound platform at York Road, looking towards central London in its final days. A young lady sits on a bench reading, but otherwise little appears to be happening.

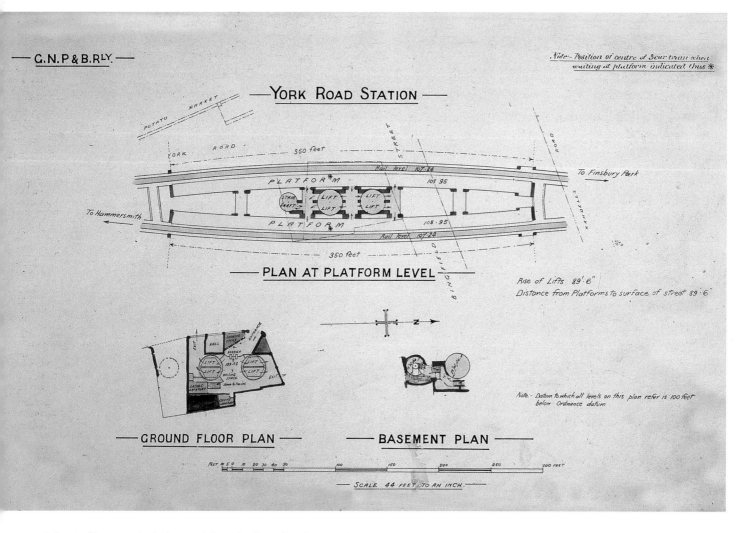

— YORK ROAD STATION —

POTATO MARKET

YORK ROAD

350 feet

Rail level 107.24

108.95

To Finsbury Park

PLATFORM ✱M

STAIR SHAFT

LIFT / LIFT

LIFT / LIFT

To Hammersmith

PLATFORM ✱M

108.95

350 feet

Rail level 107.24

STREET

BINGFIELD

RANDELLS ROAD

— PLAN AT PLATFORM LEVEL —

Rise of Lifts 89'.6"
Distance from Platforms to surface of street 89'·6

WALL

BOOKING OFFICE

LIFT / LIFT 131.46

LIFT / LIFT

WAITING SPACE

LADIES LAVATORY

EXIT

Note:- Datum to which all levels on this plan refer is 100 feet below Ordnance datum

— GROUND FLOOR PLAN —   — BASEMENT PLAN —

FEET 50 0 10 20 30 40 50   100   150   200   250   300 FEET

— SCALE 44 FEET TO AN INCH —

Below Looking towards Finsbury Park from the disused station at York Road, with the former signal box on the right.

replaced that at York Road, although the latter was not officially taken out of commission until 25th April 1964, when the signal box was also closed.

A section of platform tunnel has been bricked off from the running lines, but the remainder is still visible. The vast majority of tiling has been painted out, although a few small sections have not been touched. The signal box also survives, with its windows blackened after years of disuse.

Up above, the street level building had been leased since the 1930s to the Victor Printing Company, but later became derelict. In 1989 however, it was generally tidied up, and the removal of some boards on the facade revealed the remains of earlier lettering, including the station's name.

Above left At platform level, most of the tiling has been painted over, but fragments of wall still display the original scheme as shown here.

Above right and below The street level building, which still survives in 2021. After closure in 1932, the raised lettering on the frieze was chiselled off so that the lessees, the Victor Printing Company had a flat surface on which to fit their new signs. These remained in position until the premises were vacated, and were removed around 1989 to reveal the remains of the earlier wording underneath.

DOVER STREET

Opened: 15.12.1906.
Street level building abandoned and station renamed Green Park with
new entrances in Piccadilly: 18.9.1933.

Dover Street was one of the original stations on the Great Northern, Piccadilly & Brompton Railway and opened with the line on 15th December 1906. Its entrance, designed by Leslie W. Green, was located on the east side of Dover Street and was connected to the platforms by two lifts. These were of the Otis electric type and both had a rise of 80.66ft.

The platform tiling was carried out in cream and mid-blue and both sides included three name-panels. These showed the title simply as 'Dover Street', although the later enamel bull-seyes included the bracketed suffix 'St James'. This however did not appear on tickets and does not seem to have been included on maps.

The station was always well patronised and in 1918, a platform level barrier system was tried in an attempt at controlling crowds. Similar gates were also installed at both Knightsbridge and Holborn, in addition to various locations on the Bakerloo Line, but they were not deemed successful and were soon removed.

As traffic increased it became obvious that the street level building, tucked away from the main thoroughfare, was far from ideal, so as part of the Piccadilly Line modernisation programme of the early 1930s, a replacement was planned.

Work was subsequently put into hand and on 18th September 1933, a sub-surface booking hall was opened. This was linked to the platforms by a pair of MH-type escalators, with one located either side of a fixed stairway.

The street level building was replaced by new entrances either side of the main road, with one located on a strip of park land, south of Piccadilly and the other leading from Devonshire House. As part of this transformation the station was renamed Green Park and the tiled panels at platform level were covered by posters.

Disused parts of the station accommodated LPTB office staff during the Second World War, but otherwise the building was leased out for non-railway purposes. It survived to the 1960s with Express Dairies and Lyons' teashops adjoining each other at its southern end. Down below, the platforms remained little altered, and every so often one of the old name panels would partially reappear when posters were being changed.

The building finally succumbed to demolition in the early months of 1966, when it was removed in connection with Victoria Line works. Until the end, the words 'Dover' and 'Station' could be clearly seen on its frontage, although the central section which formerly displayed 'Street' had been obliterated.

A sub-station for the Victoria Line was built in the former basement, but parts of the lengthy subways which led from the lower lift landing still survived.

The platform tiling was largely replaced around 1985, but some of the original scheme was retained within cross-passages, together with the blue tunnel 'rings' above the tracks.

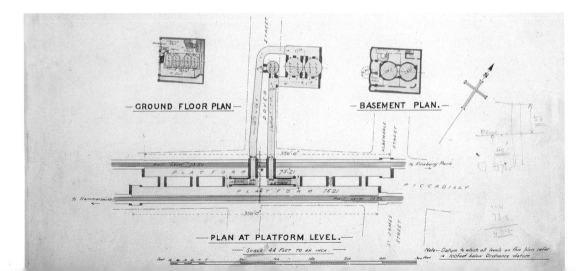

— GROUND FLOOR PLAN —   — BASEMENT PLAN. —

— PLAN AT PLATFORM LEVEL. —

— SCALE 44 FEET TO AN INCH —

Above The street level building, after a canopy had been erected over the entrance, hiding 'Dover' on its original name frieze.

Far left A platform nameboard showing the suffix 'St James'. The suffix 'Mayfair' was similarly shown on the signs at Down Street.

Left The street level building in later days, with the former entrance largely bricked-up and a teashop, owned by the Express Dairy, accommodated within the erstwhile exit.

The 'out' subway looking towards the trains. The original station tiles with their colour theme are still in good condition in much of the subway. In the distance on the right an original sign can be seen above the upper tile line indicating TO THE LIFTS. The entrance to the old subway is on an intermediate level near the stairs up from the Piccadilly Line platforms where there is a junction for passengers interchanging between the Piccadilly. Jubilee and Victoria lines. An unmarked wooden door is used for access to the subway by authorised staff.

One of the original signs on the 'in' side of the lower lift landing. The tiling theme at Dover Street was white and blue horizontal tiles with occasional vertical bands.

Through one of the lift shafts from the lift entrance. The shaft now houses a ventilation fan.

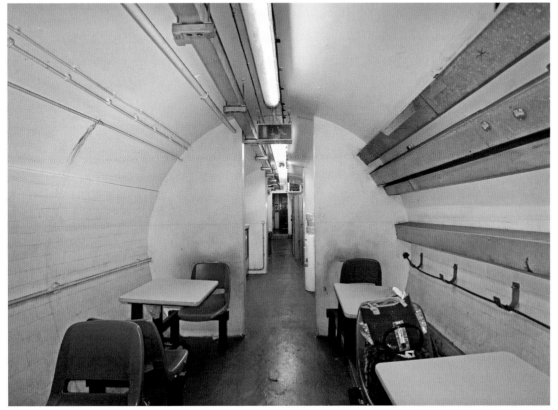

The first section of the 'out' subway has been converted into a mess room for the Green Park station cleaners. There are three rooms, the first room contains tables and chairs, the second a small kitchen and the third staff lockers. It may be this part of the subway that was used to accommodate the LT Chairman and his six Heads of Department during WW2. This is the first 'room' in the subway looking towards the lower lift landing. A door in the distance opens into the subway with its original tiling intact.

BRITISH MUSEUM

Opened: 30.7.1900
Replaced by new Central Line platforms
at Holborn: 25.9.1933.

The street level building in CLR
ownership, with signs promoting the
line as a 'Tube' very much in evidence.

British Museum station was opened by the Central London Railway on 30th July 1900, and comprised a pair of wooden platforms, each with a length of 325ft. It was located 682 yards east of Tottenham Court Road, and 746 yards west of Chancery Lane. The street level building, designed by architect Harry Bell Measures, was situated on the north side of High Holborn, on the eastern corner of Bloomsbury Court, and was connected to the platforms by means of two lift shafts. These had a rise of 69ft 8ins, and both contained a pair of lifts, which were supplied by the Sprague Electric Company of New York. From the lower lift landing, passengers descended a flight of steps and emerged at the east end of the station. There was also a stairway which led directly from the booking hall, but this was only intended for use in emergencies.

In common with the majority of other CLR stations, the street level building was constructed with a flat roof, but this arrangement was only temporary, as the company intended further storeys would be added at a later date. In the case of British Museum station, this took place when office accommodation was added above the existing structure, and leased to Messrs Colls & Sons at an initial annual cost of £270.

The tubes accommodating the station had a diameter of 21ft, and were finished in white tiling. Originally it was intended to use these on all visible areas, but to reduce costs the walls opposite the platforms were clad in matchboarding to a height of 10ft.

The station had a reversing siding at its west end, and access to this was controlled by a signal box on the westbound platform. Signalling on the CLR was initially mechanical, and worked on the Sykes Lock and Block principle. Platform starters were of the semaphore type, but were replaced by colour lights between 1912 and 1914. After the introduction of electrical signalling, a number of the boxes closed, but because of the need to control the siding pointwork, that at British Museum was retained.

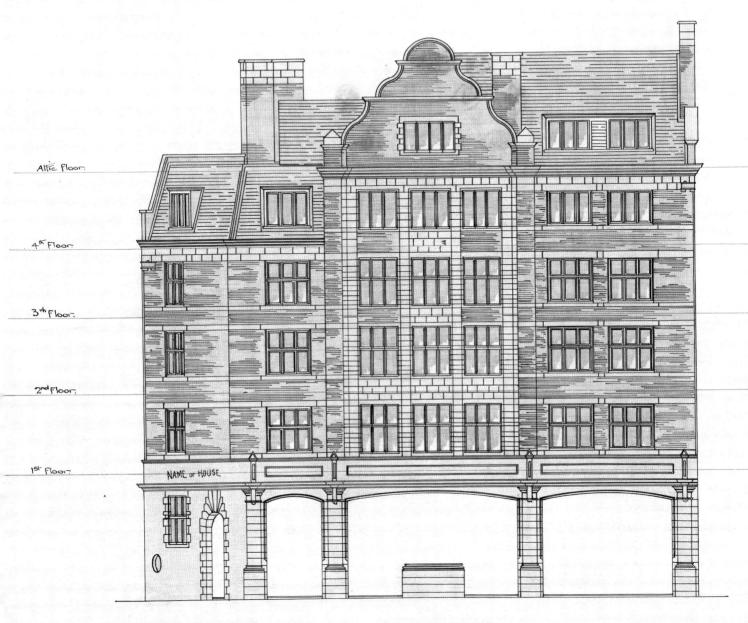

Attic Floor.

4th Floor.

3rd Floor.

2nd Floor.

1st Floor.

NAME OF HOUSE.

FRONT ELEVATION.

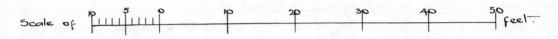

Scale of 10 5 0 10 20 30 40 50 feet.

Approved on behalf of The
Central London Railway Cº
subject to the contract and the
rights and powers of all other
authorities and Persons

Signed Harry B. Measures

Signed Allan Vigers

30/3/04.

27th April 1904.

A platform view of the station taken at an unknown date, but thought to be shortly before its closure.

Following an underground fire on the City & South London Railway at Moorgate, the CLR began to reconsider the safety of its own line, and decided to phase out the use of wooden platforms. A start was made by replacing those at Bond Street in March 1909, and authorisation to change British Museum came in November of the same year.

In 1907, the CLR considered constructing a subway linking British Museum with the newly opened Holborn station on the Great Northern Piccadilly & Brompton Railway, but this failed to materialise, and although through bookings between the two companies were introduced in 1908, interchange passengers were obliged to walk from one station to the other by way of the street.

Parliamentary authority to resite British Museum to afford a better interchange with Holborn was received in 1914, but the advent of the First World War caused this to be delayed indefinitely. Fresh powers were eventually granted in 1930, and work began on constructing the new platforms. Before a start could be made on these, new, larger dimension tunnels had to be constructed around the existing tubes without causing undue delay to services, although Drage's department store had to be demolished to provide access to the working site from street level.

Before closure there was a farcical suggestion that British Museum station was haunted by the ghost of an Ancient Egyptian, and a national newspaper offered a financial reward to anyone who was willing to remain on the premises overnight.

Stories such as this no doubt inspired the 1935 comedy thriller *Bulldog Jack*, which starred Jack Hulbert, Claude Hulbert, Ralph Richardson, and the American actress Fay Wray. Much of the action took place on a fictitious disused tube station named 'Bloomsbury', which had a secret passageway leading to a sarcophagus in the British Museum! The views of the dingy deserted station are very atmospheric, but were filmed in a studio set.

The new Central Line station at Holborn was brought into use on 25th September 1933, and British Museum was closed. The signal box remained in use for a little longer, but at the end of October 1933 it was replaced by an eleven lever power frame at Holborn.

The platforms were removed after closure, and the station tunnels were used as an air raid shelter from September 1941 until the end of the Second World War.

The street level building was demolished for redevelopment in 1989, but the white tiled walls of the former station can still be seen from a passing train.

The street level building of British Museum station in its final days of operation. An arrow beneath the canopy directs Piccadilly Line passengers to the nearby station at Holborn.

British Museum station entrance as it appeared in the 1960s. It survived until 1989.

BROMPTON ROAD

Opened: 15.12.1906
Closed: 30.7.1934

Brompton Road was opened by the Great Northern, Piccadilly & Brompton Railway on 15th December 1906, and was provided with two 350ft platforms. These were positioned 71ft 9ins below the ground, and were accommodated in parallel 21ft 2½in tubes. There were two lift shafts, each with a diameter of 23ft, and both of these contained a pair of lifts. The street level building, designed by Leslie W. Green, occupied an 'L' shaped site, which fronted onto Brompton Road itself, and included both entrance and exit. The other elevation faced Cottage Place, but although similar in styling to the frontage, does not appear to have been intended as a means of access, and its small doorway may have been used by staff.

The platform tunnel walls were tiled in the style which typified the stations constructed by Mr Charles Tyson Yerkes, the financier responsible not only for the GNPBR, but also the Charing Cross Euston & Hampstead, and the Baker Street & Waterloo railways. At Brompton Road, the base colours were white and cream, and had patterns picked out in green and brown.

It was convenient for the Brompton Oratory and the Victoria & Albert Museum, but had little else within its immediate catchment area. It was close to both South Kensington and Knightsbridge stations, which were located either side, and it seems that both of these were more popular with the travelling public.

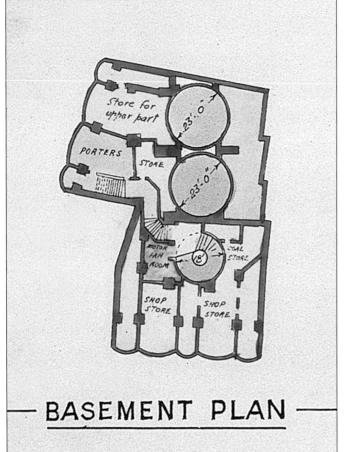

BASEMENT PLAN

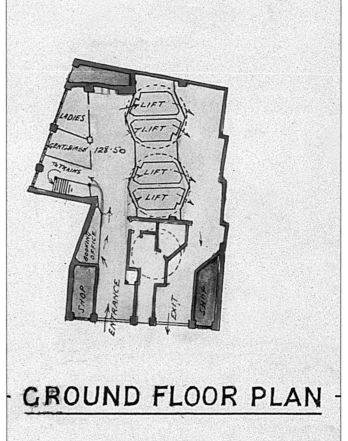

GROUND FLOOR PLAN

Brompton Road in its early days, believed to have been photographed just prior to opening.

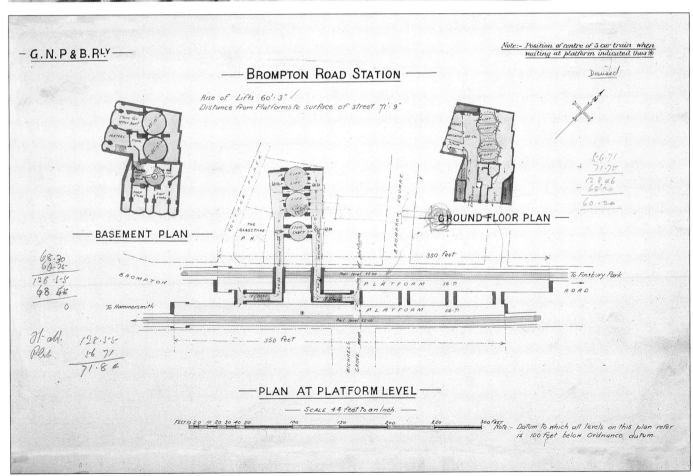

PICCADILLY
TUBE

· BROMPTON ·

This
SHOP
and Basement,
TO be LET
Agents
GARRETT, WHITE & POLAND
16, Hanover St W

WATNEY
COMBE
REID & Co
FINE
ALES

Newspapers promptly delivered

A later view of the station frontage. The public house seen earlier has been demolished for rebuilding, whilst its site hoarding provides a convenient space for advertising 'Crazy Month' at the London Palladium.

Previous page The frontage of Brompton Road station, soon after it opened. A well-dressed gent buys a newspaper form the bookstall just inside the entrance, whilst to the left a barrel organ tinkles out tunes of the day to entertain patrons of the adjoining public house.

As part of a scheme to improve Piccadilly Line running times, a practice was introduced in October 1909 whereby certain trains would pass some little-used stations, and these included Brompton Road.

The lack of patronage also resulted in a lift being removed in 1911, and being transferred to Hyde Park Corner, to increase the number there from three to four. The lift which remained in the same shaft was taken out between 1924 and 1930, and left Brompton Road with only two in operation. It was only a matter of time before further economies were made, and eventually the booking office was de-staffed, so passengers had to buy their tickets from machines or the lift attendant.

The station closed from 4th May 1926 due to the onset of the General Strike, and remained so until 4th October 1926, when it was brought back to use following questions in Parliament. At first its Sunday service was not restored, but after more debate in the House of Commons, it recommenced from 2nd January 1927.

The frustration of passengers waiting on the platform as non-stop trains hurried by had previously led to correspondence in *The Times*, and staff at either South Kensington or Knightsbridge yelling out 'Passing Brompton Road!' became so familiar that in 1928 this became the title of a play by Jevan Brandon-Thomas, which ran for 174 performances at the Criterion Theatre, Piccadilly.

JULY 12 1933

" PASSING BROMPTON ROAD "

TO THE EDITOR OF THE TIMES

Sir,—The other day I entered Dover Street Station to go to Brompton Road. The platform indicator said " Passing Gloucester Road " ; so confidently I got into the in-coming train. Immediately after there was a cry " all change," and afterwards the now empty train disappeared through the tunnel. The indicator remained unchanged.

The next train came in, and, a passenger asking: " Is this right for Brompton Road ? " doubly assured I entered it, and then I found myself at South Kensington! Hurriedly I entered a lift and changed stations for the east-bound train. There was nothing at all on the indicator and the platform was empty, save for a young porter cleaning the wall. I asked him, " Does the next train stop at Brompton Road ? " He replied: " I do not know, you must ask the guard." The train ran in ; I was in the middle of the platform, the guard at the extreme end. I called as loudly as I could: " Does this train stop at Brompton Road ? " He waved his flag, crying " Jump in," and I did so, only to find myself at Knightsbridge!

Again I changed platforms, telling my troubles to an official, and was assured that " indicators frequently got out of order."

The next train in passed Brompton Road, but the next took me safely there, 23 minutes exactly from Dover Street and 13 minutes late for my appointment!

My daughter, coming from Holborn the same day, had the same experience, and ours cannot be isolated incidents. A word in your mighty paper might remedy things, for there are few of us who have spare time to indulge in Tube jaunts.

Yours truly,
NOEL FARQUHARSON.
31, Dover Street, W.1, July 10.

By the early thirties the station's days were numbered, and following the opening of a new entrance at Knightsbridge, Brompton Road was closed from 30th July 1934.

STATIONS OF THE UNDERGROUND

No. 4. Brompton Road Station

SOUTH KENSINGTON AND BROMPTON ROAD STATIONS both serve the South Kensington Museums, but the former is nearer to them as a whole, whilst Brompton Road is just as convenient for the Victoria and Albert Museum alone to passengers journeying west by the Piccadilly Tube. Then Brompton Road Station is convenient, too, for the quiet residential byways that lie between the Brompton Road and the Kensington Road, and for Alexander Gardens, Egerton Crescent, and Egerton Gardens on the south. Other features served by Brompton Road Station are:

VICTORIA AND ALBERT MUSEUM (Architecture, sculpture, ceramics, textiles, furniture, metalwork, glass, jewellery, paintings, etc.). Open free 10 till 5 on weekdays (till 9 on Thursdays and Saturdays), 2.30 till 6 on Sundays.

THE ORATORY OF ST. PHILIP NERI.

ST. GREGORY'S LIBRARY. (This is attached to the Oratory. It is a subscription library, and specializes in works by Roman Catholic writers.)

LYCÉES FRANÇAIS (Institut Français du Royaume Uni). (A new amenity this. It is a branch of the University of Lille, with kindergarten, as well as classes for youths and young ladies. Here one may learn French as spoken by the French, and not of the modern counterpart of Chaucer's Stratford-atte-Bowe variety.)

HOLY TRINITY CHURCH AND BROMPTON SQUARE.

HARRODS, and the other shops of the Brompton Road.

ADDITIONAL ENTRANCE
KNIGHTSBRIDGE STATION

ESCALATOR CONNECTION DIRECT TO THE PLATFORM

OPEN JULY 30th

BROMPTON RD. STATION
WILL BE CLOSED
ON THE SAME DAY

M4/474

Hidden from passing trains by a brick wall, the erstwhile station at Brompton Road still displays a fair proportion of its original tiling.

In the lead-up to the Second World War, requests were made by two government departments to use parts of the station as secure accommodation should the likely outbreak of hostilities take place. One of these was the Commissioners of His Majesty's Works & Public Buildings who wished to store art treasures from the Victoria & Albert Museum in a subway, whilst the other was the War Office. The latter was ultimately successful, and the street level building, together with liftshafts and certain passages was sold to HM Commissioners of Crown Lands for £24,000 on 4th November 1938. It was used throughout the war as the control room for the 1st Anti-Aircraft Division, and was transferred to the Territorial Army after the war ended. The building remained intact until its frontage was demolished in the early months of 1972 to facilitate a road widening scheme.

The remains at track level are hidden from passing trains by brick walls, but the section of street level building facing onto Cottage Place still survives, and is a nice example of Leslie W. Green's work.

The original features at Brompton Road are perhaps better preserved than at any other disused London tube station.

The four Gun Operations Rooms (GOR) built into lift shaft No 2 at Brompton Road controlled the heavy anti-aircraft guns of the Inner Artillery Zone. GOR 4 seen here was located in the well of lift shaft No 2. The heavy anti-aircraft guns for South London were controlled from here. GOR 3 which controlled the heavy anti-aircraft gun for north London was located above this room. The ladder on the right provides emergency escape from/to GOR3. The two lift openings lead onto the lower lift landing and the emergency stairs which also give access to the three GORs above. Behind the photographer in the now blocked lift opening a surviving Cassini War Office large scale map of South London and North Surrey shows the heavy anti-aircraft gun sites of the Inner Artillery Zone South.

The section of street level building facing onto Cottage Place in 1973. Since the previous year this has been the sole part of Brompton Road station to remain above ground. It was used for armed services cadet training until 2013 and was sold by the MoD for planned residential use the following year.

The old station building on Brompton Road as it appeared in 1966. The lettering below the arched windows identifies the building as being in use by the Territorial Army and the entrance door is open.

The remains of the emergency stairs at Brompton Road. The tiling throughout the station was carried out by the firm of W.B. Simpson & Sons. Simpson's were based in St Martin's Lane and, in conjunction with the firm of A.W. Maw, were responsible for tiling a number of Yerkes' stations, including the Holborn – Brompton Road section of the Great Northern, Piccadilly & Brompton Railway.

A cantilevered walkway from the spiral emergency stairs leads into Gun Operations Room GOR 3 in the lift shaft. Note the original wall tiling still in place. The spiral stairs continue to the lower lift landing from where there is access into GOR 4.

OSTERLEY PARK & SPRING GROVE

Opened: 1.5.1883
Resited: 25.3.1934

The street level building in the first decade of the twentieth century.

Osterley was one of the original stations on the Hounslow & Metropolitan Railway route from Mill Hill Park (now Acton Town) to Hounslow, and was opened with services provided by the Metropolitan District Railway on 1st May 1883.

It consisted of two platforms, and was entered by way of a street level building on the west side of Thornbury Road. As some trains were expected to terminate there, locomotive run-round facilities were located to the west of the station, and these were controlled by an adjoining signal box on the up side. This was equipped with a mechanical frame, and was recorded in September 1905 as having eleven working levers and eight spare.

When opened, the station was surrounded by open country, and even by the 1890s very little development had taken place. To its north lay Osterley Park, whilst to the south was an estate of villas known as Spring Grove. This had been developed by one of the H&MR directors, Henry Daniel Davies, but although started in the early 1850s, its progress was slow.

Seemingly the station was always indicated on MDR tickets as 'Osterley', but the large board over the entrance carried the name 'Osterley Park & Spring Grove'. Whether this was also shown at platform level as well is uncertain, but from photographic evidence it is clear that the later platform name signs showed just plain 'Osterley'. Whether this variation was the result of an official renaming does not appear to have been recorded, but as the tickets indicate otherwise, it seems unlikely.

After Hounslow Town station reopened in 1903, down trains would arrive at Osterley and be split. Having done this, three coaches continued to Hounslow Town, and the remaining five were taken to Hounslow Barracks. In the opposite direction, two trains would set off from their respective termini, and join into one at Osterley. The spare locomotive would then proceed to a siding connected to the run-round loop and wait its next duty. Following electrification in 1905 such moves were no longer necessary, and Osterley returned to its role of a wayside station.

In the suburban boom which followed the First World War, the district finally began to develop, and the Underground encouraged this with its publicity. By 1926 patronage had grown to such a level that the station was handling a million passengers annually, and with the additional traffic generated by the extension of Piccadilly Line services in 1932, it was felt major improvements were necessary.

As part of a modernisation scheme for stations on the Hounslow branch, Osterley Park & Spring Grove was to close, and be replaced by new premises 280 yards to the west, with an entrance facing the Great West Road. This new station, with its tall tower, opened on 25th March 1934.

The former Osterley Park & Spring Grove lay basically intact until 1957, when the stairways were removed, and platform awnings were taken down. The street level building in Thornbury Road survives however, and for many years has been in use as a shop.

A platform view of the first Osterley station, looking towards central London on a very gloomy 31st December 1930.

The disused station at Osterley & Spring Grove, looking towards the rear of the street level building and Central London. It is understood that the stairs and platform awnings survived until 1957, but no photographs showing the station intact after closure have been seen by the author.

ST MARY'S (WHITECHAPEL ROAD)

Opened as St Mary's (Whitechapel): 3.3.1884
Renamed St Mary's (Whitechapel Road): 26.1.1923.
In both cases, the suffixes were not always shown in brackets
Closed: 1.5.1938

Opened on the Metropolitan & Metropolitan District Joint Line as 'St Mary's (Whitechapel)', the surface building stood on the south side of Whitechapel Road, almost opposite the junction with what is now Davenant Street. The site was previously occupied by 'Megg's & Goodwin's Charity Almshouses', and adjoined a place of entertainment known as The New East London Theatre. Although the construction of the station was funded by the Met & MD companies, it was actually built by the East London Railway.

'The Whitechapel Extension of the East London Railway' consisted of a double track formation, 27.48ch long, which linked the ELR north of Shadwell, with the Met & MD line at St Mary's. It was constructed within a 25ft wide tunnel, which had concrete side walls, with either brick arches or girders above. Because of a difference in levels between the two routes, the line was built on an incline, and for a stretch of 11.92ch it featured a gradient of 1 in 50. The sharpest curve encountered was 8ch, and in the interests of safety, this section was provided with check rails.

St Mary's (Whitechapel) station comprised two platforms, of which the westbound incorporated an open space at its rear for ventilation purposes. Both sides were linked to the street level building by means of a lattice iron footbridge, and the roof was supported by cast iron columns.

The street level building at St Mary's, Whitechapel, before it was engulfed by the Rivoli Cinema.

The station was provided with its own signal box, although this was only small, and contained just four working levers. A larger cabin was located at the junction with the ELR, and this was equipped with twelve levers. These facilities remained in use until the advent of electrification, when they were replaced by a new power box at Whitechapel.

St Mary's station and the connecting line were inspected on behalf of the Board of Trade by Major General Hutchinson on 1st March 1884, and were brought into use two days later.

As the Met & MD route was not yet ready for traffic, the first trains to serve St Mary's were provided by the South Eastern Railway, and travelled from Addiscombe Road, Croydon, by way of the spur off the East London Line. These used St Mary's as their London terminus, and operated for seven months between 3rd March and 30th September 1884. After this they were replaced by through Metropolitan and Metropolitan District services, although because some of the intermediate stations were still unfinished, these ran as empty stock between St Mary's and Bishopsgate or Mansion House. This arrangement proved to be short

lived however, as from 6th October 1884, the line's facilities were brought into full use, and passengers were carried throughout. Five days earlier, the ownership of the spur from the East London Line, or 'St Mary's Curve' as it became known, was transferred from the ELR to the Met & MD Joint Committee.

Also on 6th October 1884, a new 15.97ch double track line was opened from just east of St Mary's to a terminus above the existing East London Railway station at Whitechapel. This was known initially as 'The Whitechapel Terminus Railway', although from the outset it was the property of the MDR. Because the new premises were so close to St Mary's, a scheme was drawn up in 1887 to replace both of them with a single station. Two sets of plans were produced, but neither became a reality, and St Mary's and Whitechapel remained in use.

From 10th November 1884, the Metropolitan and Metropolitan District Railways established a service pattern of half hourly trains over the St Mary's Curve to and from the East London Line. Of these, the Met services ran into the SER station at New Cross, whilst the Metropolitan District used the nearby ELR terminus.

The station entrance after being re-signed, but completely dwarfed by the adjoining Rivoli. The view must have been taken around 1936, as the cinema was promoting Albert de Courville's film 'Seven Sinners', starring Edward Lowe and Constance Cummings, which was released that year.

A great deal of the station still survives at track level, although the walls erected to separate wartime shelterers from passing trains still hide much of the platforms. This view, taken on 25th January 1996 includes the remains of the footbridge and some of the 'Egyptianesque' roof columns which are topped with lotus style capitals.

The same service pattern was retained until the Met & MD Joint Line was electrified in 1905, when the District service onto the East London Line was withdrawn. From 3rd December 1906, the Metropolitan through trains were also taken off, and the St Mary's Curve was closed to passengers. However, this was not to prove permanent, as following an Act obtained in 1912, the ELR was electrified, and Metropolitan services onto the East London were resumed from Monday 31st March 1913.

For the majority of its existence as a passenger station, St Mary's led an uneventful life, and changed little with the passage of time. Weekend traffic was sufficiently low for it to be closed for a period on Sundays, but all-week opening was restored from 1921. The adjoining theatre went through various guises before being totally rebuilt as The Rivoli Picture Palace in 1921.

From 26th January 1923, the station was renamed St Mary's (Whitechapel Road), and although this change was displayed on the frontage, it was not implemented on tickets. No photographs of the platforms prior to closure are known to the author, so the exact wording carried on the nameboards is uncertain, and may have been simply shown as 'St Mary's'.

The station was closed from 1st May 1938 and its platforms used to store materials for the resiting of Aldgate East which was then under way. The new Aldgate East was provided with entrances at both ends, and that to the east was regarded as a replacement for St Mary's.

In the spring of 1940, the Stepney Borough Council reached an agreement with the London Passenger Transport Board whereby they were granted tenancy of the disused St Mary's station, so that it could be used as an air raid shelter. Before this was possible however, a number of structural alterations had to be made to ensure the premises were suitable for their new role, and the council agreed to cover all necessary payments.

To protect shelterers from the adjoining running lines, eight-foot high walls were erected along the platform edges, and a false concrete ceiling erected as insurance against falling masonry. The street level building was to have some of its windows bricked up and a baffle wall added at its western end, but whilst these works were under way, it was severely damaged by a bomb on 22nd October 1940, and had to be demolished.

The platform alterations continued however, and a new entrance was provided up above, but even this was to prove short-lived as it was destroyed in a raid on the night of 19th April 1941.

Traffic over the St Mary's Curve was drastically cut from 4th May 1936, and further reduced on 20th November 1939. With the war at its height, it was withdrawn completely from 6th October 1941, and although still shown on Underground maps for another six years, it was subsequently used for empty stock movements only. After the war, the site of the former street level building became wasteland with ragwort growing from the rubble, but two brick shelter entrances on the opposite side of the road survived into the 1960s, and were presumably still connected to the eastbound platform below.

Today, the site has been redeveloped, and absolutely nothing of the old station survives at street level. Down below however, the platforms remain visible, although much is hidden behind the eight-foot high screen walls. On the westbound side at least, some of the facilities installed during 1940 remain untouched, including benches, and part of a ventilation system, but the existence of these makes it very difficult to envisage the station as it once was. The cast iron roof columns survive, as does part of the old lattice footbridge, although the stairs which once served this are thought to have disappeared around the time of conversion in 1940.

The demolition of St Mary's station after being hit by a bomb on 22nd October 1940.

ALDGATE EAST (OLD STATION)

Opened: 6.10.1884
Resited to east: 31.10.1938

Originally intended to be named 'Commercial Road', this station was opened by the Metropolitan & Metropolitan District Joint Railway, 30ch west of St Mary's, Whitechapel on 6th October 1884.

The building stood on the north side of Whitechapel High Street, just west of the junction with Goulston Street, and was initially an unassuming single-storey affair.

The first Aldgate East station comprised two platforms, of which the eastbound measured 355ft, whilst the westbound was 377ft. However 40ft of the latter extended into the tunnel and could be dangerous at busy times as it had a width of just 2ft. A signal box was provided, and this stood at the City end of the eastbound platform, immediately west of the stairs from the booking hall.

When the line was electrified in 1905, it was found that the platforms were too short to take the new eight-car trains operated by the MDR, and passengers travelling in the last vehicle had to walk through to the one in front if they wished to alight. This of course resulted in delays, and as the station was close to a junction, there could be serious knock-on effects with other services.

From 1912 onwards, consideration was given to undertake improvements, and proposals were made to extend both platforms to a length of 400ft. The works were subsequently authorised, but as the two companies could not agree on funding, they were never started.

Up above however, the original street level building was demolished, and replaced in 1914 by a more impressive two-storey edifice designed by the District's architect, Harry Wharton Ford. It was built around a steel frame, and was clad in buff glazed terracotta. The booking hall, which included a small Finlay's tobacconists, was located on the ground floor, and was entered by way of two openings at the building's east end. The remainder of the lower level was occupied by a Lyon's teashop, whilst 'Smoking Rooms' were provided upstairs. Around the top of the building was positioned a prominent frieze listing some of the more important destinations served by the two railways, together with a curved pediment which showed the companies' initials and the word 'UndergrounD'. This was an early use of the namestyle with the larger 'U' and 'D' which was later to become very familiar, and was claimed by Ford as being his own brainchild.

Apart from this, very little happened, and the operational disadvantages of Aldgate East had to wait until the advent of the London Passenger Transport Board before remedy.

When the LPTB wanted to increase the length of Metropolitan Line trains to eight cars instead of six, the inadequacies caused by under-length platforms again came to the fore. However, this time the situation was exacerbated by the layout of the Aldgate triangle, which had insufficient space between the junctions to accommodate extra vehicles. As it would not have been possible to carry out the necessary alterations by retaining the original premises, it was decided to close the existing station, and open a completely new one a little further east.

Whereas the original Aldgate East had a conventional street level building as means of access, its replacement was designed to incorporate two sub-surface booking halls. To allow the necessary headroom for these, the trackbed adjoining the new platforms had to be lowered by approximately seven feet, and gradients constructed at either end to bring it up to its previous level. On the western side this needed to be 1 in 52, whilst to the east a slope of 1 in 40 was required.

Before all this could be done however, the section of tunnel which would accommodate the new station had to be enlarged, and a main sewer diverted. Firstly, a mass concrete retaining wall was constructed along the north side of the site, and stanchions added to support the new station roof. Following this, a similar operation was carried out on the south side, and the original tunnel arch could then be demolished.

Despite the fact that everything had to be done outside service hours, the new station progressed very well, and by the end of October 1938, all was ready for the final changeover. An invert was completed between the new walls, and the tracks relaid on a series of wooden and steel trestles, which could easily be dismantled when required. This meant that the running lines were virtually on a level with the new platform surfaces, so that passengers on passing trains looked down on them.

For the first time since the project began, the line had to close for a day as the engineers, working with a gang of nine hundred men, faced the herculean task of lowering around 1,400ft of double track, and demolishing the old platforms. Earlier in the proceedings, substantial eye-bolts had been fixed into the tunnel roof above the new station, and wire cables suspended from these to support the track. Once all was ready, the trestles were pulled away, and the track was lowered into its new position. The temporary wooden platforms at the old station were then demolished, and the new junction installed.

With the task now more or less complete, the new Aldgate East opened for traffic on 31st October 1938, and its predecessor closed.

The street level building in Whitechapel High Street remained in a very derelict condition into the 1950s, when it was removed to provide space for a row of shops. These have in turn been demolished, and the site is once more undergoing redevelopment.

Remains at track level include the spans of two footbridges and lotus-headed roof columns, but only the latter are visible from passing trains. There is still evidence of the resiting to be found elsewhere however, including a section of original running tunnel, abandoned when the junction was realigned, and this can be clearly seen from the south end of Aldgate station on the Circle Line. Some rather more obscure relics survive at the present Aldgate East, in the shape of the metal eye-bolts which supported the track during reconstruction, and still affixed to the tunnel roof.

Facing page upper Harry Wharton Ford's distinctive street level building at Aldgate East, which dated from 1914

Facing page lower The first Aldgate East station in 1938, showing the platforms rebuilt in wood to assist removal when the changeover took place later in the year.

The remains of the original Aldgate East, looking east with the current station illuminated in the distance. As can be seen, both footbridge spans survive, as do the original roof columns, but the platforms have been largely demolished. The photograph was taken from the District Line, with the Hammersmith & City tracks hidden behind the row of columns on the left.

UXBRIDGE

Opened: 4.7.1904
Resited: 4.12.1938
Sometimes referred to as
'Uxbridge (Belmont Road)'

From the late 1870s onwards both the Metropolitan and Metropolitan District Railways expressed a desire to serve Uxbridge, but for various reasons the schemes failed. The interest of the two companies never waned however, and eventually the Met succeeded when the Harrow & Uxbridge Railway Act was approved by Parliament on 9th August 1899.

Construction was carried out under the direction of the company's new engineer, Mr E.P. Seaton, and the firm of Bott & Stennett were appointed as contractors. Site offices were placed near Stanley Road, Roxeth, and work commenced on 9th September 1901.

Initially it was intended to carry the line on embankment between Roxeth and Rayners Lane, but the cost and impracticality of building this across marshland resulted in the erection of a viaduct instead. This, together with a cutting at Park Road, Uxbridge, was the only major civil engineering work on the branch, but even so, construction proved comparatively slow.

The terminus at Uxbridge was situated off the south-eastern side of Belmont Road, and consisted of two 473ft platforms. The main building stood on the down side, and incorporated all the usual facilities, together with a small refreshment room. Prior to the route being authorised, there had been plans to extend it towards High Wycombe, and although these had faltered, the premises were laid out for easy conversion into a through station, should the need arise at a later date.

By January 1904, the platforms and main building at Uxbridge were more or less complete, but the track had not been laid. Within six months however, everything was ready, and the line was inspected by the Board of Trade in June. To test the standard of engineering, four locomotives were operated up and down the line, with two on each track. One of these, 'B' class 4-4-0T No. 50, hauling two coaches, had a seat fixed to its front end, and the inspecting officer, Major J.W. Pringle, rode on this whilst the tests were being carried out.

The exterior of Uxbridge station, at the foot of the short approach off Belmont Road.

The line was sanctioned for opening and the ceremonial first train ran between Baker Street and Uxbridge on Thursday 30th June 1904, hauled by 0–4–4T No. 1. The locomotive was bedecked with flags, and evergreens, and left no doubt that the opening was regarded as a very special occasion. On arrival, the invited guests transferred to a large marquee outside the terminus, and sat down to a celebratory banquet.

For this event, both Uxbridge and the sole intermediate station, Ruislip, were festooned with bunting, but the introduction of regular services, a few days later on 4th July, was a much more low-key affair.

The terminus at Uxbridge was of course provided with run-round facilities, and a signal box, which housed thirty-five working levers and five spare, was positioned just beyond the ramp at the London end of the down platform. The station entrance was accessed by means of a sloping approach road, and passengers wishing to reach the up side, did so by using a transverse section of platform which lay immediately beyond the buffer stops. In contrast to the fine main building, which was constructed of brick, the shelter serving the up line was very small and was built almost entirely from wood.

Although initially worked by steam, the Act of 1899 included powers for electrification, and by the time of opening, the conductor rails were already in place. From the end of November 1904, electric trains began operating between Neasden and Uxbridge for staff training purposes, and public service commenced on 1st January 1905. For the first few months both Uxbridge and Ruislip stations were illuminated by oil lamps, but electric lighting had been installed from the outset, and was eventually brought into use once the current was switched on. In addition to its passenger terminus, Uxbridge was also provided with a seven-acre goods yard, which included warehouse facilities, together with private sidings for the wholesale grocer, Alfred Button.

Although a connection was laid between the branch and the Metropolitan District Railway at Rayners Lane in 1904, no regular trains were introduced over it until 1st March 1910. The MDR then continued to serve Uxbridge until 23rd October 1933, when the service was taken over by the Piccadilly Line.

A number of improvements were carried out on the Uxbridge branch in the 1930s, and these included the construction of a completely new terminus. The original station, tucked away off Belmont Road was not particularly well-sited for the town centre, so the decision was made to replace it with one facing the High Street. Various schemes were considered, but in the end, a design by Adams, Holden & Pearson in collaboration with Leonard H. Bucknell was accepted.

A general view of Uxbridge station, looking towards Harrow in the 1930s.

A Metropolitan Line train stands at the old station, as a train of Standard Tube Stock awaits departure from the other platform.

Right Map showing position of old and new stations as published at the time of the change

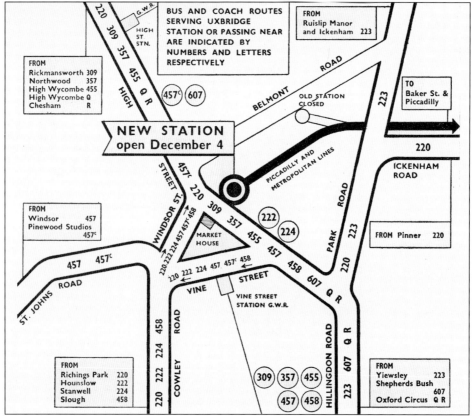

After closure, the trackbed was filled in to around platform height, but otherwise the station remained little changed.

By the early 1960s however, the platforms had largely disappeared due to further infilling and the area beneath the canopy had been enclosed. Surprisingly, the little wooden shelter opposite the main building was still standing at the time, and can just be seen, partially obscured by the foliage to the left.

The new station opened on 4th December 1938, and the original terminus was closed, although traffic continued to use the goods yard until 1st May 1939.

The track was subsequently lifted, but the station continued to stand, and was later used by the grocery business of Alfred But-ton. Towards the end it provided warehousing for a frozen food chain, but was eventually demolished to provide a site for cash and carry premises. These were removed around 1985, and the area was finally levelled to provide a car park for a large supermarket which was then under construction.

LORDS

Opened as St John's Wood Road: 13.4.1868
Renamed St John's Wood: 1.4.1925
Renamed Lord's: 11.6.1939
Closed : 20.11.1939.

The original street level building at St John's Wood Road, with the supplementary booth used during the cricket season seen on the right. Spiers & Pond's refreshment room was to the left of the station entrance, behind the window with the decorative blind.

The station was opened as 'St John's Wood Road' on 13th April 1868, and was situated 56ch from Baker Street. It was initially a passing loop on the 1 mile 76.16 chain single track Metropolitan & Saint John's Wood Railway, and comprised two platforms. That on the down side measured 297ft 8ins, and was provided with a Saxby & Farmer equipped signal box at its London end, whilst the other had a length of 314ft 7ins. These were sited in open cutting, and were covered by a glass and iron arched overall roof. The platforms were originally constructed of wood, but were rebuilt in concrete around 1905 to avoid potential fire hazards following the introduction of electric trains to the route.

The street level building stood on the south side of St John's Wood Road, close to the junction with Park Road, and was a single-storey structure built of yellow stock bricks.

The line was eventually doubled, being inspected by Colonel Yolland on behalf of the Board of Trade in June 1882. Between St John's Wood Road and Baker Street 16.13ch of new track had been laid whilst between St John's Wood Road and Marlborough Road the length was 35.50ch. Although basically happy with the standard of workmanship, Colonel Yolland requested various alterations to pointwork, and also stated that the signal box at St John's Wood Road was located too close to the platform edge.

In addition to serving the local area, the

station was conveniently placed for Lord's Cricket Ground, and therefore in summer months could be extremely busy. In fact, the small booking hall, with a width of just 11ft found it difficult to cope at these times, so in June 1892, a wooden hut was erected within the cricket ground itself for the issue of Metro-politan Railway tickets.

To the left of the street level station building was a refreshment room leased to Spiers & Pond Ltd, whilst to the right was a shop, which ended its days as a tobacconists. The latter was clearly the result of a later alteration, and resulted in the entrance canopy being reduced in width.

With the advent of the Manchester Sheffield & Lincolnshire Railway extension to London, contractors' trains needed to use the Metropolitan line to reach the building site which later became Marylebone station. To enable them to do this, a temporary junction had to be installed near the Baker Street end of St John's Wood Road, and a series of sidings laid to the west of the formation. In preparation, around 100yds of tunnel was removed, and the signal box rebuilt. This now had twenty-two working levers and

three spare, and when inspected for the Board of Trade by Lieutenant Colonel Addison in October 1895, he recorded that these were all 'correctly interlocked'. Although he was satisfied that the new box could be brought into immediate use, the pointwork leading to the temporary junction had not been connected to it, so he felt a further visit was necessary. In fact, he returned twice, and it was only after his third inspection in April 1896, that he agreed all was well. For all this, the lifespan of the junction was just over two years, as on 9th November 1898, the Metropolitan Railway informed the Board of Trade that traffic to the sidings had ceased, and that the associated points, crossings and signals had been taken out, therefore allowing operations at St John's Wood Road box to return to normal.

By 1914 the station was suffering from the effects of bus competition, and a report of that year implies that it was beginning to look rather run-down. Although repainted just eighteen months earlier, the stairways were flaking badly, whilst the platform walls were very grimy and needed re-pointing. Apart from a few illuminated signs, the station was still

The name of the station, displayed on a seatback, was reduced almost to insignificance by the overwhelming display of vitreous enamel advertisements which were fixed onto wooden boarding hiding the lower section of the retaining wall.

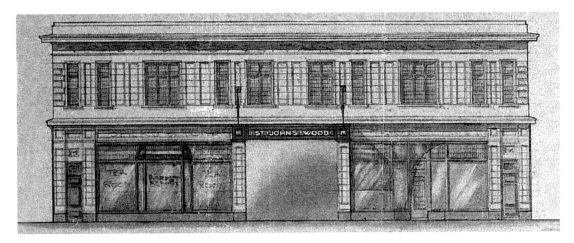

entirely lit by gas, and the report recommended the removal of the 'old fashioned gaslamp' above the entrance as it did little to improve the overall appearance.

Everyday patronage may have been gradually dropping off, but during the cricket season, St John's Wood Road station was becoming busier than ever. So busy in fact that another auxiliary booking office was constructed, although in this case the structure was portable, and was transferred to Drayton Park in the autumn to assist when Arsenal Football Club was playing at home.

This continued in use for some years, but by the 1920s, something better was evidently needed. Since opening, the station frontage had been partially obscured by a ventilation shaft, which although necessary in steam days, was now no longer required. On 12th April 1923, approval was given for this to be demolished, and replaced by a wooden booking office. In writing to the Marylebone Town Clerk, the Metropolitan's General Manager, R.H. Selbie, assured him that this would be of a 'very temporary character inasmuch as we are considering the entire reconstruction of the station building.' Work on demolishing the walls surrounding the old shaft and covering the resultant hole was soon in hand, and all was ready for the 1923 cricket season.

By this time the rebuilding scheme was being discussed in detail, and the company architect, Charles Walter Clark, was instructed to draw up plans for a new street level building. This was to incorporate space for shops on the ground floor and a design was presented for consideration in February 1923. From a surviving drawing, it appears the building was to have an oval floorplan, similar to that employed at Great Portland Street, but this

was rejected, as the company felt it needed something larger. They decided to increase the site area by extending over the space formerly occupied by the ventilation shaft, but before this could be done, authority was needed from the local Council, as a road widening scheme was thought to be in the offing, and this may have made the scheme unrealistic. In fact, after consultation, the Metropolitan Borough of Marylebone wrote to Selbie and told him that they had no objections, providing the new building was set back 10ft from their proposed improvement line.

Clark produced further drawings, but this time the design was based on a rhomboidal plan. At street level there would be a new Spiers & Pond refreshment room to the left of the entrance, and a shop to the right. Behind this were a couple of kiosks, and the new ticket office. This was to be much better equipped than its predecessor, and have six main issuing windows. Two other windows were to be provided at the rear, although these faced onto the exit passageway from the down platform, and were only intended for use in emergencies. Up above, on the first floor, provision was made for two flats, both of which were to have their own private doors and tradesmen's entrances incorporated into the building.

As part of making the site more lucrative, an iron and concrete mezzanine floor was to be erected above the platforms, and used to provide several lock-up garages. The main entrance to these, which included the attendant's office, was from the north side of Lodge Road, but additional access was also available through a gateway adjoining the station frontage.

The entire rebuilding scheme, which also included the installation of electric lighting, was initially estimated at £9,500, but by the

C.W. Clark's street level building of 1924–25, seen soon after completion. One of the entrances to the garage which was built above the platforms around the same time is visible to the left.

time tenders were invited on 2nd January 1924, the anticipated cost had risen to £14,000. Of the eleven companies requested to submit estimates, the choice fell on W.J. Maddison Ltd of St John's House, 124-127 Minories, and the contract was let on 24th July 1924. The price was to be £12,558, with completion expected in thirty-nine weeks, although after discussion with Selbie, the company agreed to reduce this to thirty-five.

Work started on the rebuilding and, at the same time, advertisement hoardings, which had been placed over wall recesses down below were removed to provide more platform space. In March 1925 tenders were invited to have the building painted, and all work was completed by October the same year.

Clarke's building was grafted on to the original and boasted a frontage clad in white faience tiling. This was similar in style to that previously used by Clark at Farringdon & High Holborn, and soon became familiar elsewhere on the system. Above the entrance was a red-painted metal canopy, which displayed the station's name on its sides, and the legend 'Metropolitan Railway' together with the initials 'MR' on the front. These were displayed in stencilled lettering, against an opaque glass background and were illuminated from behind. Near the top of the building was a frieze which featured lettering

punctuated as appropriate with small diamond symbols. These reflected the design of platform nameboard employed by the company, and also gave the shape to the mounting of a double-faced clock which was positioned above the entrance. 'Rusts' tiling was liberally used for internal cladding, and this appeared on both the booking office front, and the stairways. As the refreshment room was larger than before, the General Manager of Spiers & Pond Ltd agreed to pay an extra £150 per annum, which brought his yearly rental up to £575. The shop incorporated into the frontage comprised 336 sq ft, and according to a letter dated 21st June 1923 was to be offered to a tobacconist for an annual rent of £150. To this was added further revenue, which came from the pair of kiosks and a bookstall. The latter was operated by W.H. Smith & Sons, whilst the others were used by a confectioner and a fruiterer.

The two first floor flats varied in size, with the largest being offered for £100 per annum, and the smallest for £65. The latter was fairly basic, with living room, kitchen, bedroom and bathroom, but the larger included an additional bedroom, together with a room for the maid.

The underside of the garage floor above the platforms effectively placed the station within a tunnel, and resulted in the loss of natural daylight. The original overall roof was retained however, and having been

The garage accommodation constructed above the station as part of its mid-1920s rebuilding. A mezzanine floor was added for the purpose, but the glazed overall roof was retained.

A photograph showing remedial work being carried out on 25th January 1936, following the discovery of a crack in the retaining wall. The platform extension added to allow the operation of eight-car trains is shown to good effect, together with a Metropolitan Railway diamond type nameboard, which curiously displays 'St John's Wood Road', despite having been officially renamed St John's Wood eleven years earlier.

completely re-glazed, provided shelter for the cars underneath. The garage accommodation consisted of individual spaces encased in wire mesh on metal frames, and organised in two rows. Access to these was from a central corridor which stretched from the entrance in Lodge Road to the rear of the station building. The provision of cages seems a rather elaborate way of demarcating the spaces but some, at least, appear to have had doors for security. The modernised station was renamed St John's Wood by the Metropolitan Railway on 1st April 1925, although directional signs in the cricket ground continued to show the earlier title until the following spring.

Despite all the work however, overcrowding remained a problem during the cricket season, and in August 1925, the company were again seeking improvements. The Australian team were due to visit in 1926, and it was felt that the newly rebuilt station was unlikely to cope with the demand. Even with six booking windows in action, the queues would be horrendous, and little help could be expected from the two supplementary windows at the office rear. Unfortunately, the passageway that these adjoined was fairly narrow, and could easily become a veritable bottleneck. Therefore it was decided to build an extension to the existing ticket office, and move the windows around to the front.

At the same time the Metropolitan Railway asked the authorities at Lord's Cricket Ground if they would allow a larger hut on their site, but this request was refused because of lack of space. This hut had two issuing windows, and thought was given to increasing these to three. However, as there was only sufficient space inside for a pair of clerks, the idea was dropped, and the only changes made were largely cosmetic.

Apart from the cricket season however, business at St John's Wood was slack enough for the station to have its opening hours reduced, and from 1st October 1929, weekday trains called after 9.40am only. Local residents organised a petition against both this, and similar treatment meted out to Marlborough Road, but the company stood by their decision.

As part of a scheme to increase the length of trains to eight cars, the Metropolitan implemented a programme of extending its station platforms, with the additional sections at St John's Wood being constructed at the Baker Street end.

In 1935 Powers were granted for the LPTB to construct an extension of the Bakerloo Tube from Baker Street to Finchley Road, and thence over the former Metropolitan Railway route to Stanmore. This would bring relief to the existing line which had to contend with handling a heavy flow of traffic, particularly at peak times. One of the new Bakerloo stations was to be known as Acacia Road, and occupy a site between the existing stations at St John's Wood and Marlborough Road on the Met. In 1936, with this in the offing, the Marylebone Cricket Club suggested that the name of St John's Wood Road be changed to Lords, but although the LPTB agreed, they said that the renaming would not take place until the new tube line had opened. As the decade drew to a close, work on the new project was well advanced, but with the gathering clouds of war, some of the men engaged in construction were transferred to civil defence work, so there was an inevitable delay.

However, the LPTB finally agreed to go ahead with the renaming, and on 11th June 1939. St John's Wood station became Lords. Unfortunately, its life with this title proved to be very short as when the new line finally opened on 20th November of the same year, both Lords and Marlborough Road were closed, and technically replaced by the nearby station on the Bakerloo. By now, the LPTB had decided on a name change, and having appeared on maps as both 'Acacia Road', or just plain 'Acacia', it eventually opened as St John's Wood. Originally it was intended to retain Lords, and open it as required to serve important cricket matches, but hopes of this were dashed by the onset of the Second World War.

The platforms survived into the postwar era still displaying their nameboards, but piecemeal demolition followed not long after. The street level building lasted into the late 1960s, but has now gone without trace. A modern stairway has been constructed on the former down side for use as an emergency exit, but little else remains, and passengers peering into the gloom of the tunnel have now no obvious reminders of a station which was once so busy in the cricket season that less than eighty years ago it merited a major rebuild.

Cleaning-up operations at the disused Lord's station on 16th November 1940, following an air raid.

The south end of the station on 11th January 1945, with a very grubby 'Lords' bullseye sign still in position. The name on this has been covered over, but the lower panel, reading 'For Lord's Cricket Ground', remains visible.

MARLBOROUGH ROAD

Opened: 13.4.1868
Closed: 20.11.1939

Marlborough Road opened on 13th April 1868, and was located 1m 23ch from Baker Street on the Metropolitan & Saint John's Wood Railway. This route was originally constructed with a single track, and the station provided one of the passing loops. It was located in open cutting, and a curved iron and glass overall roof was used to shelter the two platforms. That on the down side was 259ft 10ins long excluding ramps, and had a signal box at its London end, whilst the up was 9ins shorter.

The street level building was constructed of yellow stock brick, and stood at the corner of Finchley Road and Queen's Grove. It was similar in appearance to those at St John's Wood Road and Swiss Cottage, and in common with these a Spiers & Pond refreshment room.

To speed up services, pilotmen were introduced around 1874, to act as human single-line tokens, and pass from one locomotive footplate to the other when trains crossed at St John's Wood Road. Following this, the second track at Marlborough Road was abandoned for a while, and the signal box closed.

Although nominally independent, the line was worked by the Metropolitan Railway from the outset, and this title appeared on the earliest tickets. It was finally absorbed by the larger company from 1st April 1882, and in the same year the formation was doubled throughout. The widening resulted in 35.50ch of new track being laid between Marlborough Road and St John's Wood Road, and 27.25ch in the opposite direction towards Swiss Cottage. Although not quite finished, the work was inspected by the Board of Trade in June 1882, and brought into use a month later on 10th July.

The line saw its first public electric trains on 1st January 1905, but this brought no significant changes to Marlborough Road station, which remained largely unaltered throughout its existence.

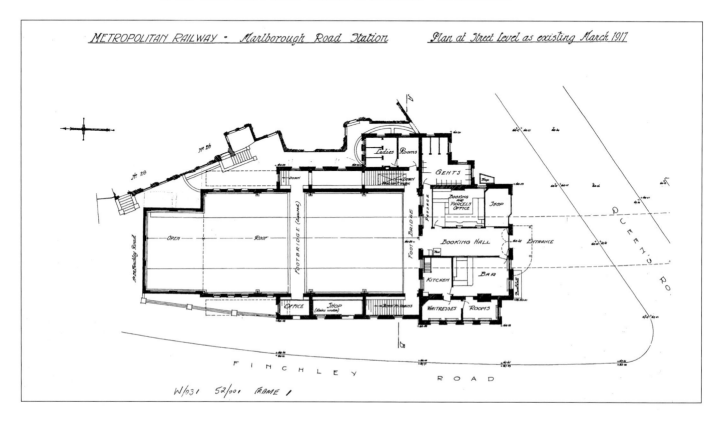

By the second decade of the twentieth century, its fortunes were suffering from 'bus competition, and the traffic levels had seen a significant decline. When Marlborough Road was subject to a Company inspection on 18th September 1914, it was recorded that figures were particularly low, and that only around forty passengers were using the station daily. This figure was perhaps a little misleading however, because at the time 'buses working between West Hampstead and Plumstead on Route 53 were being diverted because of works in Abbey Road, and proved more convenient than normal for local residents.

To improve local awareness, the Company decided to erect directional signs on lamp posts outside the Eyre Arms Assembly Rooms, which were used for concerts and dances, and were located about five minutes walk from the station. This probably did little to assist its flagging fortunes however, and in the interest of economies, the original booking office was replaced by a 'Passimeter' on 29th November 1928. Passimeters were designed for one man operation, and were located in positions where a single clerk could both issue and collect tickets. This rendered the existing ticket collectors redundant, and therefore reduced the station's wage bill.

Despite this however, Marlborough Road seemingly remained unremunerative, and together with St John's Wood Road (See Lords), was subject to heavily reduced opening hours from 1st October 1929. The chief reason for doing this however was operational, as the two tracks between Baker Street and Finchley Road could become very congested at busy times, and it was calculated that if both stations were closed during the morning peak, twenty additional trains could be worked through to central London.

Not that this impressed the local residents however, as a Mr S. Goetze received 131 signatures on a petition against this partial closure, and sent it to the Metropolitan Railway's General Manager, Mr R. H. Selbie on 18th October 1929. The petition asked 'Why should the St John's Wood and Marlborough Road Districts be made to suffer owing to the Metropolitan Railway's policy of making systematic and sustained efforts to develop outlying districts ... Why should these two districts be entirely deprived of their train service during the morning 'rush' time, because the Metropolitan Railway has boomed Metroland ... Not very long ago the Metropolitan Railway placed outside Marlborough Road station, an attractive advertisement, in which it drew attention to its excellent service from that station citywards:- '8-3 8-13 8-23 etc. Remember the 3's' ... Does it feel justified in having thus endeavoured to make City workers settle in that District, only to leave them soon afterwards with a station closed to them till an hour when, for most of them, it is practically useless.'

Selbie replied on 30th October, and stated that the decision to close both stations until 9.40am and after 5pm was only reached after careful consideration, and it was intended to improve conditions for suburban passengers who were totally reliant on the railway when travelling to or from work. As locals had seemingly favoured buses of recent years, he suggested that they continued using that means of transport, and not use either station as a means of commuting.

The seeds were now clearly sown for permanent closure, and it is perhaps surprising that both Marlborough Road and St John's Wood managed to survive for another decade.

Despite their bleak future however, both had their platforms lengthened in the early 1930s, so that they could take eight-car trains. When this had been completed, the up side at Marlborough Road was increased by 97ft 4ins, whilst the down received an extension of 50ft 6ins.

The death blow for both came when the Bakerloo Line was extended from Baker Street to Finchley Road, and a new tube station was opened at St John's Wood. This was regarded as a replacement for both of the earlier Metropolitan establishments, and they were both closed from 20th November 1939, when the new service commenced.

Marlborough Road station is understood to have survived the war years largely intact, but by the 1960s was showing the effects of nearly three decades of disuse. The platforms had been partially demolished, but the ironwork of its overall roof survived until around 1967, albeit devoid of glazing. For many years, the large brackets which once supported this were still in position, but these have recently disappeared.

Fortunately however, the attractive street level building has survived, and having lain derelict for a while, apart from a small section which housed a doctor's surgery, it became a restaurant in the early 1970s, and although having changed hands, remained as such for many years.

The street level building at Marlborough Road, with the entrance beneath the canopy to the right. Adjoining this, behind the bookstall, is the open window of Spiers & Ponds refreshment room.

SWISS COTTAGE (MET)

Opened: 13.4.1868
Closed: 18.8.1940

The street level building of Swiss Cottage station seen here about twenty years before it was rebuilt by C.W. Clark.

Swiss Cottage station was constructed as the terminus of the single track Metropolitan & Saint John's Wood Railway and was provided with a street level building on the west side of Finchley Road.

It was situated 1m 61ch from Baker Street and comprised two platforms. Excluding end ramps, that on the up side measured 296ft 6ins, whilst its opposite number was fractionally longer at 298ft 2ins. A signal box was provided at the far end of the down platform and was fitted with a Saxby & Farmer frame. As with St John's Wood Road, the platforms were originally wooden but were rebuilt in concrete around 1905.

The station was opened for traffic on 13th April 1868 and, although used as a terminus, a single line continued for 156yds beyond the platforms as part of a proposed extension to Hampstead. This was not to materialise in its intended form, but in the late 1870s it was incorporated into what later became the Metropolitan main line to Rickmansworth, Amersham and beyond.

Work on this started in 1878, but was delayed by bad weather. Between Swiss Cottage and Finchley Road a cut and cover tunnel had to be constructed, and a long section of viaduct was needed on the approach to Kilburn. The contractor, Joseph Firbank, had men working around the clock on the latter to ensure the line was ready in time for the 1879 Royal Agricultural Society's Show at Kilburn, but he didn't succeed. The line from Swiss Cottage to West Hampstead opened on 30th June 1879, with the stretch to Willesden Green following five months later on 24th November.

The Saint John's Wood company was officially absorbed by the Metropolitan Railway in April 1882, and by June of the same year the single track sections between Baker Street and Swiss Cottage had been doubled.

Now it was no longer a terminus, Swiss Cottage settled down to the life of a through station. A Metropolitan inspection held in September 1914 recommended various economies, including removal of the Station Master and replacing the ticket collector with a relief

porter. The inspector was also critical of the booking office staff, who were described as *'fairly smart, but not fully conversant with Season ticketing arrangements.'*

As part of a modernisation programme implemented by the Metropolitan after the First World War, Swiss Cottage became a prime candidate for improvement. In a letter to the Company Estate Agent dated 15th June 1925, the General Manager, Mr R.H. Selbie stated *'This station, as you are aware, is in a very obscure position and in need of rebuilding with a view to giving the entrances greater prominence and, if possible, utilising some of the waste space on the site ...'*

A little earlier, the architect Charles Walter Clark had been asked to prepare a new design, and this was duly presented for consideration. The old stock-brick street level building would be largely swept away, and its place would be taken by an arcade, constructed to the same 18ft width as one already in use at Liverpool Street. The original building of 1868 accommodated a Spiers & Pond refreshment room, and although this was to be retained more or less in its existing position, it would be extensively remodelled to suit its new surroundings. The arcade would generate extra money for the Company, by providing seven shops, and three kiosks. In addition, a block of three railway-owned shops which faced onto Finchley Road could be demolished, and the relevant businesses relocated into the new premises.

The booking hall would be positioned at a lower level, and an additional entrance was to be provided from Belsize Road, although Clark felt that in addition to increasing the cost of reconstruction, some of the kiosks would have to be less favourably placed.

Above the shops on the west side of the arcade, a three storey block of flats was to be constructed, and as the platforms would now be completely in tunnel, new, more effective electric lighting would have to be installed instead of the gas which was then in use.

One small obstacle which needed to be removed however was an adjoining building, Nos 123/5 Finchley Road, which since June 1882 had been leased to the Saward family, and used as an umbrella shop. The building, which also included living accommodation, was owned by the railway, and had to be demolished as its site would be absorbed by the arcade. The property was valued at £1,500, but to ensure it would be vacated with the minimum of fuss, Selbie offered the Misses Saward compensation of £3,000. He also suggested that they might like to take one of the new shops on a twenty-one year lease, for an annual rent of £50, and this they accepted.

The Belsize Road entrance to the station, with a sign directing passengers to the sub-surface booking office visible inside.

Since Clark's original drawings had been produced, various alterations had been made, including the addition of a passimeter booking office, and reduction of the arcade's width to 16ft, but by the end of 1927 the Company were ready to invite tenders. Nine building firms supplied estimates, and on 23rd February 1928 the job was awarded to the Pitcher Construction Co Ltd of Hornsey Road, who promised completion within fifty-six weeks, at a cost of £30,702. Obviously the overall plan had still not been finalised however, because in May 1928 an alteration was approved which resulted in an additional storey being added within the mansard roof of the flats. This was estimated to increase the construction cost by £2,800, and would provide four flats instead of three as originally intended.

During July 1928, with work in its early stages, the proprietor of a local grocer's shop was unhappy with the disturbance and began writing letters of complaint to the railway. The first concerned vibration, and requested that speed be reduced on the down line, whilst the second, which was possibly the main cause of dissatisfaction, regarded a hoarding which was obscuring his premises. However, by the autumn, much of the old street level building had gone, hoardings had been erected all around, and a temporary entrance was provided through the rear of the former estate office. On 21st September 1928, a 12ft 9in x 4ft 3in sign was erected above this stating '*Metropolitan Railway. Entrance to Swiss Cottage Station for Booking Office and Trains to Baker Street, City & West End.*'

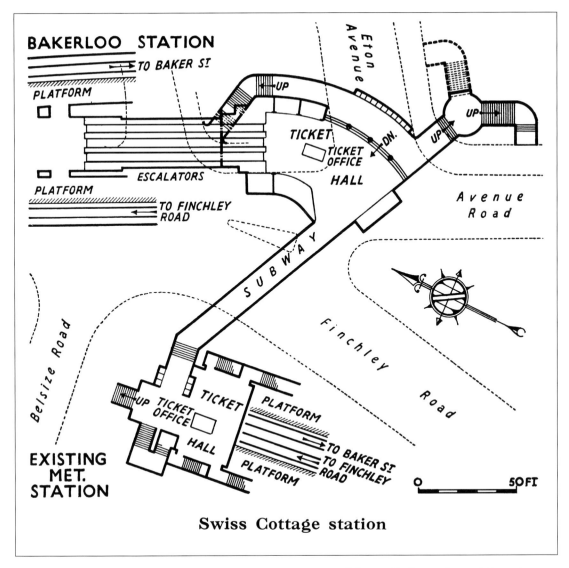

Swiss Cottage station

At around the same time, the Metropolitan was in the process of extending its platforms to take eight-car trains. At Swiss Cottage, the rather narrow extensions were added at the Baker Street end, and provided a further 53ft 3ins on the up side, together with 83ft 7in on the down.

By the following year, the project began to take form, and the finished station, sporting a new white faience frontage, was ready by 30th September 1929.

With the advent of the Bakerloo Line extension to Stanmore in 1939, Swiss Cottage was the only Metropolitan station between Baker Street and Finchley Road which was to be retained. It was to become an interchange, and a subway was to be built connecting it with the new tube premises. The latter was to have its ticket hall beneath the surface of Eton Avenue and Avenue Road, and be connected to street level by two stairwells.

Despite the construction of the subway and ticket hall however, the interchange between the Metropolitan and Bakerloo Lines at Swiss Cottage proved to be short-lived, as the earlier station closed from 18th August 1940, and was never reopened.

The arcade at street level continued in use, and provided an additional entrance to the Bakerloo, but this was eventually demolished in the late 1960s.

At the time of writing, remains of the two platforms can still be seen from a passing train, together with an exit on the down side which has been retained in case of emergencies.

KING'S CROSS, ST PANCRAS (MET OLD STATION)

Opened: 10.1.1863
Metropolitan and Circle Line platforms resited: 14.3.1941

The original Metropolitan Railway station at King's Cross was opened with the line on 10th January 1863 and had its entrance on the east side of Grays Inn Road. From here, passengers descended to the platforms, which were protected by an overall glass and iron roof with a span of 80ft.

The earliest trains to serve the route were provided by the Great Western Railway. These operated between Bishops Road, Paddington and Farringdon Street and were of the old GWR 7ft broad gauge.

The two tracks to the south of the formation were intended for the use of both broad and standard gauge services, whilst a third, which lay to the north was standard gauge only. This was used by up trains off the Great Northern Railway, which accessed the Metropolitan by means of a connection known as The Eastern Branch or York Road Curve. Their counterparts travelling in the opposite direction operated over the down mixed gauge line then diverged a little to the west of the station onto the steeply graded Hotel Curve which brought them out alongside King's Cross main line terminus.

The Metropolitan station was provided with four platform faces, of which the central pair took the form of an island. Those on the south side served the mixed gauge tracks, whilst the others were located either side of the standard gauge line. This arrangement did not last long however, as the Metropolitan Railway (Additional Powers) Act of 25th July 1864 authorised the final stretch of what became The City Widened Lines between King's Cross and Moorgate Street. So that construction could proceed, GNR services was suspended from 1st July 1867 and not restored until early in the following year. In July 1868, they were joined by trains off the Midland Railway, which reached the route by way of a link from St Paul's Road Junction, north of St Pancras.

The layout of the Metropolitan station at King's Cross was altered to accommodate an extra track to the north of the formation.

Because of restrictions imposed by the site, this could only be achieved by removing the northern side platform, and building a replacement to the east. This was staggered from the remainder of the premises and accessed by means of a footbridge. In later years, the platforms were again re-arranged, when a new up side, serving the Widened Lines, replaced that of 1867-8. This was still slightly staggered, but was more conveniently positioned than before. For this to be done, the island had to be reduced in width and may have undergone minor lateral resiting, using space on the Metropolitan side made vacant after broad gauge workings ceased in 1869.

For many years, passengers wishing to interchange with the main line terminus at King's Cross had to cross busy main roads, but a direct subway connection from the west end of the Metropolitan station was opened on 20th June 1892 and subsequently extended to provide connection with the Great Northern Piccadilly & Brompton Railway.

Further changes came during 1911–12, when the original station entrance was removed to make way for a new road, known as King's Cross Bridge. This was constructed in connection with London County Council tramway improvements, and as it stretched above the west end of the platforms, also resulted in the overall roof being removed. Separate entrances for the Metropolitan and Widened Lines platforms were erected a short distance from each other on the south side of Pentonville Road, with the former being a building, designed by Frank Sherrin, located at the junction with King's Cross Bridge. From here, passengers descended to a circulating area where a new booking hall was provided.

By this time, the old Metropolitan station was beginning to prove inconvenient, particularly since the advent of what are now the Piccadilly and Northern Line tubes in 1906 and 1907 respectively. Nevertheless, the situation remained unchanged until after the formation of the London Passenger Transport Board,

The King's Cross Bridge entrance of the Metropolitan King's Cross Station in 1933, situated at the top of Grays Inn Road opposite the Scala cinema. A new King's Cross station complex was part of the 1935–40 New Works Programme.

when better interchange facilities at King's Cross became an essential part of central area integration.

Although the station would remain open for Widened Lines services, the platform faces on the Metropolitan side would close and be replaced by new premises about 250 metres to the west. Work on this commenced early in 1936, but was delayed by the onset of war as the decade drew to a close. The new complex was to have a sub-surface booking hall, with subway connections to both King's Cross and St Pancras main line termini, as well as having entrances in Euston Road. The new tube booking hall was brought into use on 18th June 1939, but the Metropolitan premises were still unfinished. This is perhaps not surprising, as engineers had to widen the existing formation to take two completely new side platforms, which flanked a bay at their western end.

The Blitz brought a great deal of disruption to the area and the project took on a new urgency when the original station received air-raid damage. Enemy action resulted in Metropolitan services being suspended from 16th October 1940 and although subsequently restored, they only ran intermittently for a number of months. Nevertheless, work on the new facilities somehow continued and although unfinished, they were officially opened on 14th March 1941.

There can be little doubt that the new station, known from the outset as King's Cross St Pancras, was much better located than its predecessor, and had a far greater interchange potential. Nevertheless, the central bay at its western end, which was intended for eastbound terminators, was never brought into use, and was largely filled-in at the start of the 1960s to provide an enlarged circulating area between the two side platforms.

By this time, the earlier station had taken on a very run-down appearance, with its bare, empty platforms and grimy retaining walls, relieved only by 'King's Cross St Pancras' roundels on the Widened Lines side. It had opened simply as King's Cross back in 1863, but became King's Cross & St Pancras in 1925, and lost its "&" in 1933. Therefore, both this and the new premises to the west carried the same name, which must have led to confusion amongst those who were unfamiliar with the area.

The steam hauled suburban trains linking the former Midland and Great Northern systems with Moorgate continued to call, as did the diesels which replaced them, but the other side remained dead and all Underground services passed through without stopping. Paper stickers had been pasted onto the rear wall of the westbound side, with the legend 'Station Closed' displayed in black Johnston type on a white background, but although some of these had become torn with the passage of time, they remained clearly readable. The eastbound platform, which was formed from the southernmost face of the central island, was devoid of such signs, although it was segregated from the open part of the station by a fence.

The former Metropolitan Railway station at King's Cross, looking towards Farringdon in the spring of 1934. We can be certain about the date, because the courtroom drama 'Libel!' which is advertised on the poster at top right, opened at the Playhouse Theatre on 2nd April that year and starred Montreal born Frances Doble as "Lady Loddon". Amongst the cast was a young Alec Guinness, who was then making his stage debut. The abandoned platform can still be clearly seen today from a passing train.

The Widened Lines side of the station on 24th August 1938, with LMSR Class 3MT 2-6-2T No 35 arriving with a Moorgate – East Ham train, which was routed via Kentish Town, South Tottenham and Woodgrange Park. On the opposite side of the island platform can be seen an eastbound service formed of ex-Metropolitan Railway stock.

At street level, the building of 1911–12 was largely turned over to commercial premises, although London Transport retained part of it for departmental use. Further west along Pentonville Road, the little entrance which provided separate access to the Widened Lines platforms, continued to serve its intended purpose and displayed a British Railways Eastern Region blue nameboard upon its frontage.

The services to and from the old Great Northern system ceased from 5th March 1977, leaving just those off the Midland to serve Moorgate for a little longer. These were withdrawn on 14th May 1979 and the remaining section of

the old Metropolitan Railway's King's Cross station was closed, but this was not to be the end. It reopened as King's Cross Midland City on 11th July 1983 and assumed its final name, King's Cross Thameslink, on 16th May 1988. For its reopening, a new, spacious booking hall was constructed on the site of the earlier Widened Lines entrance, but the 1911–12 street level building by the junction with King's Cross Bridge remained as before. This continued to provide staff access to the old Metropolitan Line platforms below. Stairways, partially clad in green tiling, led to both sides, but although the westbound survives more or less unaltered, most of the eastbound had been incorporated into the rebuilt King's Cross Thameslink which backs onto it. As part of a scheme to improve interchange and other facilities, new low level platforms were subsequently provided at St Pancras International and these were brought into use on 9th December 2007, when King's Cross Thameslink was closed.

After closure, the 1980s entrance to Kings Cross Thameslink was retained as access to the Underground system by way of subways, but the 1911–12 Metropolitan Railway street level building at the corner of King's Cross Bridge has been demolished.

WOOD LANE

Opened: 14.5.1908
Closed: 23.11.1947
Sometimes shown on early tickets as
Wood Lane (Shepherd's Bush)

On 26th July 1907, the Central London Railway received Parliamentary authority to extend passenger services beyond Shepherd's Bush, and to build a new station at Wood Lane to serve the Franco-British Exhibition. This would be accommodated at the north-western corner of an existing depot site, and be served by a single-track loop.

Westbound trains would continue beyond the former terminus and use the original steeply graded line to bring them to the surface beside the depot. From here, new track would need to be laid, to take them to Wood Lane station, then into tunnel for their journey back to Shepherd's Bush. This would burrow beneath a section known as the Caxton Curve, then join up with the existing reversing siding. Having completed their anti-clockwise trip around the loop, trains would continue on the eastbound line, and return to the City.

Apart from serving the exhibition, it was felt that the new line would have operational advantages, as trains would no longer need to shunt on arrival at Shepherd's Bush, but just run out to Wood Lane, then return without reversal.

The architect, Harry Bell Measures FRIBA was employed to design the new station, and drawings were forwarded to the Board of Trade for approval. Measures had previously designed the stations on the original section of the Central London Line, together with those grim bastions of Victorian philanthropy known as Rowton Houses, which were erected between 1895 and 1905 to accommodate homeless men.

By the beginning of 1908 it seems that little work had been done at Wood Lane station, as the Board of Trade were unhappy with the submitted design. They wrote to the CLR on 29th January stating that the platforms, which were to be 15ft wide, might prove too narrow to deal with crowds, and that there were insufficient toilet facilities available. In addition they were concerned that no awnings were indicated, and therefore the station appeared as if it was to be open to the elements.

The company replied two days later, explaining that an elevated covered way leading from Uxbridge Road to the exhibition site would be above the platform and concourse areas of the new station, and would therefore afford passengers with adequate shelter. They also mentioned that the stairways would be roofed with light corrugated iron, and although details were still not finalised, they assured them that the lavatory accommodation would be adequate. This seemingly satisfied the Board of Trade, as on the 12th February 1908 the CLR was given the go-ahead to proceed with their plans.

Work must then have got under way very swiftly, as by 9th May Wood Lane station was ready for official inspection. Colonel Yorke RE, CB visited the premises, and reported to the Board of Trade that he was happy with the arrangements. He noted that the new section of line stretched for 43.55 chains, and was *partly in tunnel and partly on the surface*. He also recorded that its steepest gradient was 1 in 30, and its sharpest curve had a radius of 4 chains.

Having received the final blessing from the Board of Trade, the new line was deemed ready for traffic, and was brought into use to coincide with the opening of the Franco-British Exhibition on 14th May 1908.

The street level building was constructed on the east side of Wood Lane, and was provided with a separate entrance and exit. Passengers entering the station did so at the north end, then made their way onto a spacious concourse. Immediately to their right was a staircase which provided direct access from the exhibition walkway, whilst behind this lay a porter's room. The booking office was in a direct line with the entrance, and was equipped with eight ticket windows. Of these, two were at the front, and the remainder were in groups of three positioned either side. To left and right of this were a pair of 1 in 25 slopes which led down towards the ticket barriers, and allowed access to toilets. The Station Master's office was situated between the two barriers, and adjoined the east end of the ladies' room.

The original Wood Lane station frontage, as designed by Harry Bell Measures, dwarfed by the arcaded covered way which led from Uxbridge Road, Shepherds Bush, into the exhibition grounds.

Stanley Heaps' new frontage of around 1915, with Underground bullseyes created from white blue and red mosaic tesserae.

The eastbound platform 3 at Wood Lane, opened in 1920, clearly showing the steel troughing used in roof construction. The view is looking towards Shepherd's Bush and daylight can be seen near the junction with the original terminal loop. The enamel nameboards were apparently not ready by the time the photograph was taken, and posters were displayed instead. These had the name printed in a black slab-serif typeface on a white background, whilst the backing roundel appeared in a 'warm' red.

As the new extension comprised of a single track loop, there was only one line passing through the station, but this had a platform face on either side. Of these, the one immediately beyond the ticket barrier was designated No. 2, whilst the other was No. 1. This was the shorter of the pair, and was sited on the inside of the curve. Judging from Drawing H25A which was submitted by the CLR to the Board of Trade on 14th March 1908, it appears that No. 1 was intended for passengers alighting, whilst No. 2 was for those who wished to board. However, when trains were later strengthened from six to seven cars, the position was seemingly reversed, as the rear vehicle would be beyond the end of the shorter platform and of no use for anything but departures.

From the south-western end of No. 1, a flight of stairs led onto a covered footbridge over the line, and towards the station exit. This could also be accessed from the other platform by means of steps and a 1 in 16 slope. The passage widened to 16ft, and descended to street level on a gradient of 1 in 21. At the bottom was a sharp corner, and an office for the sale of exhibition tickets. This was located to the left, and adjoined a stairway which provided direct access to the overhead walkway. Those wishing to visit the event could therefore make use of this, or else leave the station by the exit onto Wood Lane, and walk across the road to the main exhibition entrance.

As referred to in the correspondence with the Board of Trade, the majority of the station was effectively roofed by the overhead walkway, although a short section of Platform 2, and a slightly longer part of Platform 1 remained open to the elements at their south-western extremities. Pointwork at both ends provided access to and from the depot, and a new signal box was positioned immediately to the east of Platform 1. This replaced an earlier structure which adjoined the original depot reception siding, and when first commissioned had twenty-one operational levers, and nine spare.

The Central London Railway lost no time in promoting its new extension, and the convenience it offered to visitors. On a contemporary poster designed by William Tomkin, it was described as 'The Direct Route To The Franco-British Exhibition', and announced that the 'Exhibition Station' was served by 'Trains every few Minutes all day'.

The Franco-British Exhibition closed on the evening of Sunday 31st October 1908, but the site was used for annual displays until 1914. It was then handed over to the Government, who used it for various purposes before vacating in the early 1920s.

From 1st January 1913, the Central London was absorbed into the Underground Group, and the new management soon set about making improvements to the line. These included the installation of automatic signalling, the replacement of some earlier trackwork, and the erection of bullseye station nameboards.

At Wood Lane, Measures' original frontage was removed around 1915, and replaced by a new design from Stanley Heaps. He had worked on the various Yerkes' projects as Leslie Green's assistant, and was appointed architect to the London Electric Railway in 1910.

The new frontage projected slightly further onto the pavement, and was finished in brown tiling. The original layout was retained, with gated entrances at either end, but above these now rose a distinctive pediment featuring a pair of Underground Group roundels, created from white, blue and red mosaic tesserae.

These alterations were comparatively minor when compared with the changes which took place a little later, when Wood Lane station was enlarged to four platforms. The reason for this was the construction of a new line, known as the Ealing & Shepherd's Bush Railway, which was built by the Underground Group and the GWR.

The ESBR had been authorised by the Great Western Act of 1905, and the Central London Act of 1911. It commenced at Ealing Broadway, then continued eastwards until joining up with the West London Railway at Viaduct Junction, and the former CLR near Wood Lane. The majority of work was carried out by the GW, but one furlong and seven chains within the vicinity of Wood Lane were built by the Underground Group. It was opened as a freight link between the Great Western and West London lines on 16th April 1917, but passenger services did not start until conductor rails were in position, and the new connections were ready at Wood Lane.

Because the station had originally been laid out as a single track loop, it was not particularly easy to extend, and the result produced an operating idiosyncrasy which survives to this day. Immediately beyond the tunnel mouth to the east of the depot, a junction was constructed which allowed westbound trains to take the extension. Having briefly surfaced, they then had to dive below ground level again to reach the new platform. A similar situation existed on the western side of the loop, where the eastbound track emerged from a new tunnel, and joined up with the existing formation. By adapting and modifying the earlier layout, it meant that conventional left-hand running was not possible through Wood Lane, and a flyover had to be constructed north of the station.

Col. J.W. Pringle inspected the Ealing & Shepherd's Bush Railway on 25th July 1920, and approved it for opening to passengers. In his report he made mention of the fact that both lines at Wood Lane included 1 in 31 gradients, which although steep, were not severe. The westbound route had curves which varied from 4.25ch to 6ch, but the eastbound was straight. The track consisted of 90lb bullhead rail, and was laid in 42ft lengths.

In anticipation of the new extension, various alterations were carried out at Wood Lane station, including the construction of two new platforms. Col. Pringle's report recorded that these were approximately 300ft long, and 15ft wide. They were both situated in cut-and-cover tunnels, with concrete retaining walls and roofing which comprised steel troughing, girders and concrete. That which served the eastbound line became No. 3, whilst the other was designated No. 4.

The station walls were largely tiled in white, with panels for nameboards and posters outlined in green and black. The same colour scheme was extended to the concourse, which was redesigned with greater use being made of the available space. Booking facilities were improved, and extra toilets for both ladies and gentlemen were constructed.

The two new platforms were linked to the concourse by separate entrance and exit stairways, although from the outset it was felt that under normal conditions each side would require only one of these to be in regular use.

The signal cabin was modernised, and equipped with a power-worked frame. This was provided with twenty-one working levers and ten spare. Points and signals were electro-pneumatically operated, and all roads in the station and depot were track-circuited. There was an illuminated diagram, which not only gave the signalman a clear indication of movements in the immediate vicinity, but also on the lines towards Ealing, as far as Wood Lane Junction on the Great Western section.

The signalling initially employed on the Ealing & Shepherd's Bush Railway was of particular interest as it consisted of three

Enamel name sign showing the use of the crossed version of the Johnston W.

position upper quadrant semaphores. These were automatically controlled by the track-circuiting, and some had pointed arms, similar to a style employed in the USA.

In 1927, the White City Stadium began to be used for greyhound and motor-cycle racing, and further alterations were necessary at Wood Lane station to cope with the additional crowds. The old booking office was removed, and replaced by passimeters, which had electrically operated machines, capable of issuing 20,000 tickets an hour. These speeded up the flow of passengers, and also had the advantage of creating more space.

Platform 1 at Wood Lane was incapable of taking seven car trains, so passengers had to use No. 2. However, with the introduction of sliding-door stock, this began to cause problems, as the additional doors and absence of gatemen brought about a potential danger to passengers. Being on the outside of a sharp curve, there was a considerable gap between the platform coping and the carriages, and this meant that special care had to be taken when joining or alighting from trains. Therefore, it was apparent that Platform 1 needed to be extended, although this would prove to be very difficult because of the pointwork leading to and from the depot.

In February 1928 a moveable section of platform for Wood Lane was designed and submitted to the Ministry of Transport for approval. This was to be fitted at the eastern extremity of No. 1, and swivelled out of the way when a train was running on or off shed.

This mobile platform was made of soft wood on a steel underframe, and was pivoted at its western end. It moved on rollers, and was electro-pneumatically controlled from the signal box which it adjoined. It was thirty-five feet long, and six feet wide, and at normal times was aligned with the passenger track. When necessary, the signalman could operate his lever, and the wooden extension would swivel over a distance of around 4ft, so as to clear the road serving the depot.

The movement was activated by No.10 lever in the signal box, and powered by two point cylinders working in parallel. After swivelling in either direction, the platform was bolt locked into position, and this could be done by operating lever No.9.

At the time of the Ministry's inspection, the signal box had twenty-three working levers, and eight spare. The illuminated track circuit diagram remained as before, but had been altered to include the mobile platform and its securing bolt.

The report mentioned that around thirty daily movements were anticipated in and out of the yard, and that the swivelling platform might be operated up to one hundred and twenty times within twenty-four hours. The idea was undoubtedly a success, and the ingenious, if somewhat unusual moveable platform remained in use until the station closed.

With Platform 1 suitably lengthened, No. 2 was no longer required, and apparently ceased to be used for regular traffic. To improve passenger flow, a footbridge was built which led from the circulating area, and rose above the former slope to Platform 2. Having gained enough height, it crossed the track, and descended to No. 1. This was used by passengers joining trains, whilst the original was retained as a way out.

Prior to this, access was gained to the subterranean platforms 3 and 4, by means of the two stairways to the left of the booking hall, but when these were blocked by the wooden ramp leading to the new bridge, they had to be closed and replaced by two others, which had previously lain dormant. As mentioned earlier, the sub-surface platforms at Wood Lane were each constructed with separate entrance and exit stairways, but in practice, these were used for passengers passing in each direction, so only a single pair was deemed to be necessary at any one time.

There was also another means of access between the high and low level platforms. This took the form of a short subway linking the eastern ends of 2 and 4, but this was for staff only, and was not used by the public.

Apart from the neighbouring depot, it was obvious that the operating conditions at Wood Lane station were also far from ideal. It had proven difficult to accommodate seven cars in the high level platforms, and any longer trains would be impossible to handle. In 1938, the London Passenger Transport Board therefore received powers to resite the premises, but although completion was scheduled for April 1940, progress was delayed by the Second World War. The spot chosen was 350yds north of the original, and work finally commenced on 6th May 1946. To enable its construction, the cutting needed to be widened, and the westbound line was re-routed through a new 220yd covered way.

Wood Lane station was closed after the last train departed on 22nd November 1947, and its replacement was opened the following day. This was named White City, and it was situated almost opposite the Stadium.

The station remained untouched for a while, and in February 1948 it was reopened for a few hours because of disruption elsewhere on the line. Until 18th July of that year, passenger trains continued to pass through both the abandoned low level platforms and occasionally stopped to change crews. After this however, the new westbound tunnel was completed, and the line through the erstwhile No. 4 was converted into a depot approach. This was achieved by re-aligning the track to the east of the station, then bringing it up on a rising gradient, which cut across part of the old formation. The far end of the platform would have fouled this, and therefore a short section had to be partially demolished. The necessary track alterations took just over a year to complete, and the new approach was brought into use from 7th August 1949.

Immediately after closure some, or perhaps all, of the names on the sub-surface platforms were blanked out with strips of paper. These were stickers bearing the name 'Oakwood' which had been printed in connection with the renaming of Enfield West in September 1946, but pasted face down.

The high level platforms in the 1930s with the underside of the arcaded walkway from Shepherd's Bush serving as an overall roof.

The moveable section of platform 1 at Wood Lane station, with the signal box just visible to the right.

At street level, the old station premises lingered on, much as before, but soon became progressively derelict.

The section of exhibition arcade which once formed an overall roof for the high level platforms had gone by the mid-1950s, together with the imposing bridge over Wood Lane. This left the concourse virtually open to the elements, with just a lattice of rusting girders overhead to indicate where the walkway once had been.

The track which served platforms 1 and 2 was lifted, and the formation left to become overgrown. In the nearby depot various changes also took place, including the construction of a Railway Training Centre in 1963 on the site of some earlier sheds.

Occasionally the disused areas have been used in television programmes when a suitably 'creepy' old station was required, such as in 1973 when they appeared in a series of *Doctor Who*.

In June 1994, a planning application was presented to the local council, with a view to redeveloping much of the land to the east of Wood Lane as a comprehensive shopping centre, complete with car parking facilities and bus station. The street level building was demolished in the autumn of 2003, so that its site, along with that of the high level platforms could be cleared. At sub-surface level, the former eastbound platform was subsequently removed in connection with a scheme to replace the old CLR depot with a new complex of stabling sidings. These sidings were laid during 2006 and brought into use on 15th January 2007.

The site of the high level platforms was cleared, and early in the spring of 2005 the top of the covered way above the eastbound Ealing & Shepherds Bush line was partially removed, resulting in platform 3 being exposed to daylight for a time.

The remains of the high level platforms in the summer of 1966. The girders which once supported the arcaded walkway were still in position at the time, together with the derelict footbridge, and what appears to have been a couple of nameboard supports in the right foreground.

Above Part of the frontage of Wood Lane station, as it appeared in 2001. Occasionally in the past, the paint flaked away and revealed the original colours of the mosaic Underground symbols below, but these were always re-covered. The building was demolished in 2003, but one of the bullseyes is now displayed at the current Hammersmith & City Line station at Wood Lane, which opened in October 2008.

Left The remains of the concourse at Wood Lane in the early 1970s.

SOUTH ACTON

Opened: 13.6.1905
Closed: 2.3.1959

A line from Mill Hill Park (now Acton Town) to South Acton was authorised by Parliament in 1878, but the scheme was to lay dormant for twenty years. Work eventually started on it during 1898 however, and although enough space was allowed for a double track formation, it remained single until 1905. The branch stretched a distance of just 1,232 yards and was on embankment for most of its length, but there were two bridges where it passed over roads. These were constructed of steel and were provided with skew spans. The first stretched 62ft, and was located at Bollo Lane, whilst the other measured 42ft and was positioned above Palmerston Road. Near South Acton, the line joined the North & South Western Junction Railway, and a signal box known as District Junction was erected.

The route opened to freight on 15th May 1899 and was initially used by the contractor C.J. Wills & Sons for conveying materials destined for the Ealing & South Harrow Railway, which was then under construction.

Although the E&SH line had been authorised as a separate company in 1894, it was worked from the outset by the Metropolitan District Railway and in February 1902 a plan was announced whereby the route would be electrified. The new services would operate from South Harrow, through to Mill Hill Park, and then over the spur into South Acton. Work on this soon commenced, but when the electric trains started running in the summer of 1903, they all terminated at Mill Hill Park.

With the advent of Hounslow line electrification however, the spur was at last to see passenger traffic, and a single platform capable of accommodating six cars was erected behind the up side of the existing NSWJR station at South Acton.

The MDR station was technically situated on a through line, but was intended for use as a terminus. It was completely separate from its neighbour and, although the two were connected by a passageway, it had its own entrance and ticket office. The building was located at the south-western end of the platform, and was constructed from corrugated iron and wood. It included a general waiting room together with toilets for both sexes, and was protected by a short canopy. On the platform, a little beyond the building, stood South Acton signal box, which in 1905 was recorded as having thirteen working levers and two spare. The box was fitted with a mechanical frame, and controlled all operations around the station.

Passenger services started on 13th June 1905, when electric trains began operating between South Acton and Hounslow Barracks. Less than a month later, on 1st July, a train was derailed whilst entering South Acton station shortly before 05.00, and, having fouled the points, disrupted traffic for a number of hours.

By the early 1920s, the majority of trains serving the station operated at approximately fifteen minute intervals between South Acton and South Harrow, with a few of these being extended to Uxbridge. There was also a service to and from Hounslow Barracks, although this was limited to around six return trips each day.

In addition to the frequent passenger workings, the line continued to be served by freight trains, with both the London & North Western and Midland Railways having running powers over it. In time however, the number of these began to diminish and in 1930 the junction with the former NSWJR beyond South Acton station was severed. The second track was taken out of commission after 14th February 1932, and subsequently lifted, but during its final week a few Piccadilly Line tube trains operated between the Hounslow West branch and South Acton for training purposes. From 15th February, the South Acton service was reduced to a shuttle to and from Acton Town, and was worked either by a two-car set, or a solitary 'B' Stock vehicle which had been modified for the purpose. With single-line working in operation, there was no longer a need for the station signal box at South Acton, so this was closed and demolished.

The line between Acton Town and South Acton was latterly operated by Q23 Stock cars specially converted so that they could be driven from either end. The two views depict the branch terminus, whilst that to the left shows the shuttle on its short journey between stations.

Around the same time, Acton Town station was being rebuilt and a short bay platform was provided on its eastern side for the shuttle.

Just prior to the Second World War, the earlier vehicles were replaced by two 1923 Q23 Stock motor cars, which were converted so that they could be driven from either end, and for its remaining days the branch train consisted of one coach only.

From 15th June 1958, Sunday services were withdrawn, and on 18th September the same year, London Transport announced that they wished to close the line completely.

The weekday service remained very good to the end with the first train setting off from Acton Town at 06.00, and the last returning from South Acton at 23.52. In between these times the basic pattern provided a train every ten minutes, although this was improved to seven during the peak periods. The journey time was of course very short, and some members of staff referred to the shuttle as 'The Tea Run', because it was possible to get out and back in the time it took to boil a kettle!

The last services ran on 28th February 1959, with official closure taking effect from 2nd March. The track was lifted within a few months, and the station was demolished soon afterwards, but the bridge over Bollo Lane survived into the following decade. This collapsed during demolition, and blocked the road for several days whilst being cut up. One of its abutments remained standing however, and still survives, but apart from this the only tangible relic of the branch is the abandoned bay platform at Acton Town, where the single-car shuttle once waited hopefully for any passengers who wanted to join it.

WHITE CITY

Opened as Wood Lane (Exhibition) Station: 1.5.1908
Temporarily Closed: 1.11.1914–5.11.1920
when it reopened as Wood Lane (White City).
Renamed White City: 23.11.1947
Closed: 25.10.1959

To serve the Franco-British Exhibition of 1908, a new station was constructed on the Hammersmith & City Railway between Shepherd's Bush and Ladbroke Grove.

It was only intended to be a temporary affair, and was therefore constructed largely from wood. The contract was let to Henry Lovatt Ltd on 12th December 1907, and the cost was estimated to be £5,725. However the final bill came to £5,981 11s 1d, which according to the Company's papers included £7 10s for 'extras' from Harrods!

As it was erected on an existing viaduct, the job proved a relatively easy task, although the H&CR were obliged to pay compensation to two families living in MacFarlane Road, as the platform buildings would effectively block out daylight from their homes.

These problems did not delay construction however, and the new station, known as 'Wood Lane (Exhibition)' opened on 1st May 1908.

The two platforms measured about 347ft in length, and stood to a height of 3ft 3ins. They were protected by awnings, and although waiting rooms were provided on both, the facilities on the up side were more substantial, and included a gents' toilet. The ladies' room and conveniences were located down below at street level however, and adjoined the booking office. This was accommodated within an existing arch, and was accessed from the west side of Wood Lane. There was also a connecting passageway into the adjoining exhibition site, and Metropolitan Railway publicity of the time described the premises as *'The only station right in the grounds'*.

There could be little doubt that the Great Western and Metropolitan Railways did their best to publicise the station at Wood Lane. Large signs were erected on the side of the viaduct whilst directions towards the booking office were emblazoned on the inside of the arch.

Wood Lane was provided with its own signal box, and when this was inspected by the Board of Trade in June 1908, it was reported as having eleven levers, of which five were spare.

When the H&CR decided to build the station, an agreement was reached whereby the exhibition authorities and local landowners would provide a one-third subsidy towards its construction, and in return they would receive 15% of the net receipts. The exhibition authorities were also responsible for carrying out certain works at ground level, but the progress on these was slow, and on 28th May 1908, the Metropolitan Railway wrote to them complaining that the adjoining arches had not been decorated as agreed. A report of this time stated *'The passage way between the staircase to the Up platform and the Entrance Hall of the Exhibition was commenced about a week ago but no progress has since been made. The provision of this passage way would have a very beneficial effect upon our traffic and would avoid a good deal of congestion which now occurs nightly at the main exit. The Great Western Company have commenced to put up the arc lamps, but things are moving very slowly ...'*

Despite these minor setbacks, the station proved to be a success, and it remained open after the exhibition closed on 31st October 1908. Within a couple of years however, traffic began to decline, and it was missed by alternate trains between 1st November 1910 and 15th January 1911. Closure came on 1st November 1914, but the premises remained intact, and reopened

for one day as 'Wood Lane (White City)' on 5th November 1920 to serve a motor show. From then on the station was used spasmodically, but only when an event was being staged at White City stadium.

It was renamed White City on 23rd November 1947, but closed following fire damage on 24th October 1959, and was demolished two years later. Many years later, as a result of local developments, it was decided that the area again needed a station on the Hammersmith & City Line so, on 12th October 2008, the present Wood Lane was opened on a new site to the north-east of the original.

A platform level view showing the station in the 1930s. The legend 'White City' included on the nameboard is in slightly smaller lettering than the rest, because it replaced the word 'Exhibition', originally shown.

A view from street level, showing the nameboard displayed prior to the station being renamed in 1947.

TOWER HILL (OLD STATION)

Opened as Mark Lane: 6.10.1884
Renamed Tower Hill: 1.9.1946
Resited: 5.2.1967

The completion of the Inner Circle had lain dormant for many years, initially for financial reasons, and later because of the bad feeling engendered between the two companies involved. Matters were not helped when the Metropolitan Railway, under Sir Edward William Watkin, decided to 'go it alone' and build the section from Aldgate to The Tower of London.

The Metropolitan District Railway, uneasy partners in the venture, objected strongly, but this was only the latest in a string of events which had caused a serious rift in the Met & MD Joint Committee. The companies had constantly bickered, and at one time the MDR became so enraged that it withdrew from the scheme completely. Following arbitration however, the situation improved, and work started on the new line east of Mansion House. The engineers for this were Sir John Hawkshaw and J. Wolfe Barry, and the contract was let to the firm of Thomas Andrew Walker in autumn 1882.

The line took two years to complete, and received a ceremonial opening on 17th September 1884. This was purely a special event attended by the Lord Mayor of London and various other dignitaries, and the public service did not start until Monday 6th October.

The Metropolitan wanted to retain their Tower of London station, and extend it, but the MDR objected, and insisted new premises had to be built. The site chosen was 117yd to the west, and the station was to be called Seething Lane. This was later changed however, and when it opened it was named Mark Lane.

The Tower of London station remained in use for another week, but was then closed and eventually demolished.

Mark Lane comprised two platforms and had a surface building at the corner of Byward Street and Seething Lane. In 1911, the street level building was demolished and replaced by a new entrance incorporated into an office block. Other than this however, the only major change came on 1st September 1946, when the station was renamed Tower Hill.

In 1957, it was suggested that the platforms should be widened, and that they would benefit from better lighting. Unfortunately, there

The original street level building at Mark Lane, situated at the corner of Byward Street and Seething Lane.

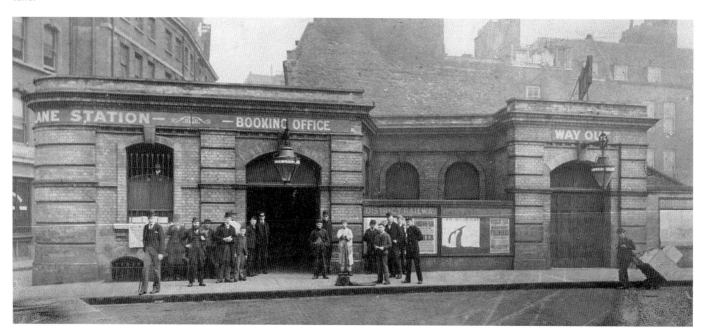

were a lot of other station improvements in the offing at the time, and those at Tower Hill were considered as less important. However, three years later, London Transport began to think seriously about closing the station, and replacing it with a new one on the former Tower of London site.

For many years the reversing of certain trains at Mansion House had caused both inconvenience to passengers and operating difficulties. In addition, the facilities at Tower Hill were falling short of public expectation, and had become a constant source of complaints. Traffic had been growing steadily since 1955, and future developments such as the electrification of the BR line into Fenchurch Street would certainly bring more commuters. The existing station at Tower Hill was in fact the nearest on the LT system to Fenchurch Street, but it was thought that the distance between them made the interchange unsatisfactory.

The scheme therefore envisaged extending the Mansion House reversing trains to Tower Hill, where the need for an additional bay necessitated the move eastwards. This would not only increase passenger capacity, but also provide a better connection with Fenchurch Street by reducing the walking time by about a third.

In readiness for this, London Transport obtained the approval of the British Transport Commission in March 1960 to lease the ground floor of an office block to be erected on the east side of Trinity Square, and therefore reserve space for the new booking hall. Following this, Parliamentary powers were sought, and the whole scheme was approved in the Commission's 1961 Act.

Within three years the plans were finalised, and on 4th November 1964 it was announced that the contract for resiting was to be let to W. & C. French Ltd at an estimated cost of £853,000. The work entailed extensive alterations at the former Tower of London site, so that the formation could be widened to accommodate the extra platform face. In addition, a sub-station above the line, and the 1914–18 Mercantile Marine War Memorial in Trinity Square Gardens both needed underpinning.

The erstwhile Mark Lane closed on 5th February 1967, and was simultaneously replaced by the new station, although much work at the latter remained to be done. Although the eastbound platform had been more or less completed, the westbound still had a temporary surface, as the trackwork needed to be altered before it could be finished as an island.

At first, the earlier station remained unaltered, but after a couple of days of closure, the engineers moved in, and demolished the westbound platform so that the points for the reversing road could be installed on the site.

The platform face which had been temporarily used by westbound services at the new station became the bay, and when the hoardings finally came down, the other side of the island was ready for through traffic. Various signalling alterations then had to be made, and on Wednesday 14th February 1968, a little over a year since the station opened, all was ready for the Ministry of Transport inspection.

There can be little doubt that the 1967 Tower Hill station is a vast improvement on its predecessor, as, in later years, the former Mark Lane was a pretty dingy place.

Its 1911 entrance remains on the north side of Byward Street, and until fairly recently it was just about possible to see the outline of the legend 'Mark Lane Station' on the stonework, although the lettering itself had long since been removed, and all that remained was a faint shadow. Apart from this, and the pedestrian subway it now serves, the old eastbound platform remains largely intact, although alterations have been made to the stairway.

The entrance to Mark Lane station, set within the ground floor of the office block erected on the site of the original street level building in 1911. To the left are the initials of the Metropolitan Railway, whilst those of the District appear to the right.

The westbound platform at the former Mark Lane station, as it appeared on 28th March 1966.

Here we see the eastbound platform as it appeared shortly before closure. Although the westbound side was subsequently demolished to facilitate track alterations, this platform still exists and can be glimpsed from passing trains a little to the west of the present Tower Hill.

A 1966 view of the street level entrance with carved reliefs on either side showing the initials of the Metropolitan and District Railways. The lettering above the arched opening to the right read "Mark Lane Station Buildings" but, like the two reliefs, this has long since disappeared.

The former entrance is seen at the centre of this view, surmounted by a blank plaque which once carried the station's name.

ALDWYCH

Opened as Strand: 30.11.1907
Renamed Aldwych: 9.5.1915
Temporarily Closed: 22.9.1940–1.7.1946
Closed: 3.10.1994

The 573 yard branch between Holborn and Strand owed its origins to a proposed scheme known as the Great Northern & Strand Railway, which was incorporated by an Act of Parliament in 1899 to relieve pressure on King's Cross suburban services between Wood Green and central London.

Unfortunately, the necessary capital could not be raised, and the scheme appeared to be doomed. However, the GNSR came to the attention of the American financier, Charles Tyson Yerkes, and he felt that it would be beneficial to amalgamate part of the route with his own Brompton & Piccadilly Circus Railway, which was then in the planning stage.

Within a year, two separate bills were presented to Parliament, and these included a new section of line to connect both schemes. The companies were officially merged on 8th August 1902, and the combined organisation became known as the Great Northern, Piccadilly & Brompton Railway three months later on 18th November.

As built, the GNPBR stretched from Hammersmith to Finsbury Park, and opened to the public on 15th December 1906, although the short branch from Holborn to Strand had to wait for nearly a year before it was brought into use. The branch was a left-over from the original GNSR scheme of 1899, and it perhaps seems strange that it was actually constructed. Prior to the work commencing, there had been two attempts to make it more useful, by extending it either to Temple or Waterloo.

In connection with the latter, a new location was deemed necessary for Strand station, and a plot was earmarked on the south side of Strand, near the corner with Surrey Street. Since 1858, this had accommodated the Royal Strand Theatre, but by the turn of the century the establishment's popularity was in decline, and it was suffering from serious financial problems. Its final production was a musical entitled *Miss Wingrove*, which only ran for a few performances between 5th and 13th May 1905, when the theatre closed. After this it was

quickly demolished, and the site acquired by the railway company.

Construction of Strand station commenced on 21st October 1905, and it opened to traffic on 30th November 1907. Its surface building followed the ground plan of the old theatre exactly, and was basically an L shape. It had entrances onto both Strand and Surrey Street, and was similar in styling to all the other stations on the GNPBR. It was designed by the architect Leslie W. Green, and featured ruby-red glazed bricks on its facades.

92ft 6ins below street level there were a pair of 250ft platforms, clad in the distinctive style of tilework adopted by the Yerkes' tube companies. However, by the time the station was being completed, it was obvious that it was only going to accommodate short trains, and therefore only a part of its walls were tiled, the remainder being left bare. The subterranean passages leading to the platforms were also tiled, as was the emergency stairway. Most of this tiling was cream, but dark green was used for decorative patterning.

At Holborn, the easternmost of the twin tunnels was provided with a 350ft platform, and had a trailing junction with the eastbound GNPBR main line, but the western track terminated at a 250ft bay.

At first the majority of trains used the eastern platform at Strand, and operated into the through side at Holborn. During peak times however, a spare train, which had been stored in the western tunnel would be brought out, and run alternately with that on the other track. Therefore although the permanent way of the branch was technically double, it was generally used in the manner of two single lines.

As the station was conveniently sited for many of the West End theatres, a special late night train was operated to take playgoers back to their suburban homes. This ran every evening except Sundays, but its popularity soon waned as it was withdrawn from 5th October 1908.

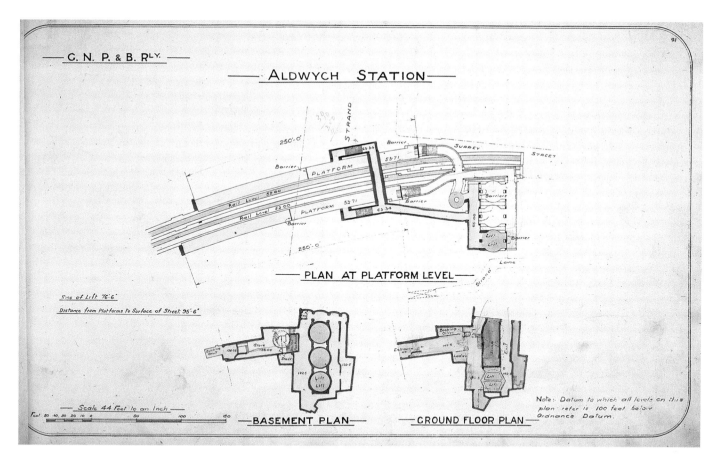

— ALDWYCH STATION —

— PLAN AT PLATFORM LEVEL —

Size of Lift 76'6"

Distance from Platforms to Surface of Street 95'6"

Scale 44 Feet to an Inch

— BASEMENT PLAN —

— GROUND FLOOR PLAN —

Note: Datum to which all levels on this plan refer is 100 feet below Ordnance Datum.

From 3rd March 1908, the off-peak branch shuttle switched to the western tunnel, although it crossed over just south of Holborn to use the eastern platform. After 1912, the other line was scarcely used at all, and it eventually fell into disuse.

From 1st July 1910, the Great Northern Piccadilly & Brompton Railway was amalgamated with the Baker Street & Waterloo and Hampstead Tubes to form the London Electric Railway.

The branch from Holborn continued to be something of a white elephant, and was scarcely used to capacity even during rush hours. Strand station was renamed Aldwych from 9th May 1915, and its tiled name panels at track level painted over.

Sunday services were withdrawn after 1st April 1917, then four months later on 16th August the eastern tunnel on the branch was officially closed, together with the east platform at Aldwych and the bay at Holborn. From 12th January 1918, the operation became 'One train on line' and soon after the crossover south of Holborn was replaced by a 15mph restricted curve.

In October 1919, there was again talk of extending the line to Waterloo, but the idea remained dormant. Traffic continued to be light, and from 17th October 1922 the booking office at Aldwych was replaced by ticket issuing facilities in the lift.

Despite the lack of patronage, trains ran all day, and operated frequently from Monday to Saturday. The line was suggested for closure in 1933, but nothing came of it and things continued as normal.

In the mid-1930s, the service operated every four minutes from 06.15 until 20.00. It then ran every five minutes until 23.58 from Aldwych.

With the onset of the Second World War it became an obvious candidate for closure, and notices were printed announcing that trains would be withdrawn from 1st November 1940. However with worsening conditions brought about by the Blitz, it actually closed a few weeks earlier, on 22nd September, and part of it was transferred to the Westminster City Council, to be fitted out as a public air-raid shelter. The bay platform at Holborn, disused since 1917, was used as offices and dormitory accommodation for staff, whilst nearby, various exhibits from the British Museum, including the Elgin Marbles, were stored in the tunnel to protect them from possible bomb damage.

The Aldwych branch reopened on 1st July 1946 and in 1948 there was yet another possibility of the branch being extended to Waterloo, but it was described at the time as being 'low priority' and again nothing happened.

Aldwych station made the headlines on 3rd August 1955 when a two-car train ploughed through the stop-blocks, injuring five people, and badly damaging its leading cab. The accident occurred at 10.54 in the morning, and the coaches were presumably lightly loaded at the time, otherwise it may have been more serious.

In the summer of 1958, London Transport announced its intention to close three of its most unremunerative stations. These were South Acton, Mornington Crescent and Aldwych. As it turned out, the last two received a reprieve, although Aldwych services had been drastically reduced. From 9th June 1958, the line operated at peak periods only, with Monday–Friday trains running 07.00–10.30, and 15.30–19.00, whilst Saturday workings were restricted to 07.00–14.00. This was further reduced from 18th June 1962, when the Monday–Friday timetable was amended to 07.15–10.15 and 15.45–19.15 and the Saturday service was taken off altogether.

In 1965 it seemed that the line was to be extended to Waterloo after all, and Parliamentary Powers were granted on 5th August that year to allow this to happen. Detailed planning took place, and tender documents were prepared, but public expenditure cuts in 1967 halted any physical work taking place and the scheme was eventually dropped.

In the meantime, Aldwych continued much as before, with just a relatively small number of passengers using it daily. Because of this, it was often hired by film and television companies who needed an Underground station for one of their productions, and in this manner it carried some pretty unlikely names. Films which feature scenes taken on the Holborn–Aldwych branch include: *The Conspirator* (1949), *The Clouded Yellow* (1950), *The Gentle Gunman* (1952), *The Collector* (1966), *Death Line* (1972), *Ghost Story* (1973) and *Superman 4* (1986).

Over the years, the derelict platform at Aldwych was used by LT design staff, and provided

Opposite The almost apologetic main entrance which faced onto the Strand, after the station had received its final name. The canopy is of an early type and includes ornamentations, presumably carried out in wrought iron.

Below left Aldwych station in use as an air raid shelter during the Blitz of 1940.

Below The crew smile for the camera, as they stand beside their two-car train of standard stock employed on the shuttle service from Holborn in the 1950s. Aldwych station was not conveniently placed to afford a connection with other Underground routes, although an illuminated sign directed passengers towards Temple on the District Line, which was a short walk away.

mock-up facilities for new station decors. In the 1960s, part of it was dressed as 'Oxford Circus' to evaluate the tiling scheme to be employed on the Victoria Line then under construction, whilst a decade later it became 'Bond Street' on the Fleet Line. The last time it was used for such a purpose was in connection with the refurbishment of Holborn, and wall panels with a '*British Museum*' theme, as adopted for Holborn, were still *in situ* in 1993.

The last chance for Aldwych to become a more useful part of the Underground system came in the 1970s, when it was suggested as an interchange with the proposed Charing Cross–Fenchurch Street extension of the Fleet Line. This was to be funded by the Greater London Council, but as luck would have it there were numerous financial problems, and the scheme failed to materialise.

The final death blow for the branch came from the need to replace the old Edwardian lifts at Aldwych station. With only around 450 people using the station each day, LUL couldn't justify the necessary £3 million, and on 4th January 1993 they announced their intention to close it. By this time, the line was running at an annual loss of £150,000, and in addition to the cost of lift renewals, a further £3.8 million would have needed to be spent on essential maintenance over the next ten years.

Approval was finally received from the Secretary of State for Transport on 1st September 1994, and the closure was scheduled for the end of the month.

By Friday 16th September, the majority of the station's enamel signs had been removed, including the two platform nameboards. At track level, blue-on-white paper LT roundels displaying 'Aldwych' had been fixed to the walls with adhesive tape, while up above, near the entrance, a vintage sign had been uncovered advising passengers to acquire tickets from the liftman or machine.

The last day was Friday 30th September, although for a while, a threatened Underground strike put this in doubt. As it happened the strike was postponed for a week, and the station opened for the final time as planned.

Above left A group of enthusiasts are seen on the long-closed platform at Aldwych during an organised visit in the 1960s. The tiling was still in fairly good condition, and included one of the original 'Strand' name panels.

Left The Surrey Street facade after closure.

With the departure of the last train, Aldwych station again became empty, as it had been for so much of its existence.

Within a week, the enamel nameboards at street level had been removed, leaving the entrance canopy looking very bare. Behind this, a panel displaying the station's original name survived, and eventually resurfaced in 1998 when the canopy was removed. At the time of writing, the street level facades remain little altered, and both continue to proclaim the legend 'Piccadilly Rly' in large black lettering.

In an attempt at cost cutting, the Holborn end of the station remained untiled throughout its existence. This view shows it shortly before closure, with the name displayed on a temporary paper sticker.

Although normally covered, or partially covered by posters since 1915, the Strand name panel on the surviving platform re-appeared in its entirety just prior to closure and was in excellent condition.

The booking hall gateline at Aldwych, as it appeared shortly before closure.

The lower lift landing at Aldwych retained some nice vitreous enamel signs, including that on the left which directed passengers to the trains.

Another view of the lower lift landing at Aldwych showing a vintage enamelled sign with a finger pointing towards the emergency exit.

Passage linking the lower lift landing to the platform in September 1992

Steps down to Platform 1 in
September 1992

Platform level signs at
Aldwych.

TRAINS TO
HOLBORN
FOR
PICCADILLY LINE
AND
CENTRAL LINE

ALDWYCH

ALDWYCH

No Smoking

Opposite The foot of
the emergency stairs at
Aldwych.

CHARING CROSS
(JUBILEE LINE)

Opened 1.5.1979
Closed 20.11.1999
but used on occasions
since official closure

The Jubilee Line station at Charing Cross, featuring one of David Gentleman's designs based on the themes of Trafalgar Square and Nelson's Column. It was one of 11 such panels designed by the artist for this station.

To accommodate the original terminus of the Jubilee Line, opened in 1979, extensive alterations had to be made at Charing Cross, including the combination of the existing stations at Strand and Trafalgar Square. The former, which was located on the Northern Line, had started life with the name Charing Cross when it opened on 22nd June 1907. It was originally the central London terminus of the Charing Cross, Euston & Hampstead Railway, but became a through station when the tracks were extended to Charing Cross (Embankment) on 6th April 1914. The earlier premises were renamed Charing Cross (Strand) at the same time, and amended to just plain Strand on 9th May 1915.

The station closed after traffic on 16th June 1973 to allow the necessary alterations to be carried out, but the changes at Trafalgar Square were less drastic, so trains continued to call whilst they were under way. Trafalgar Square, on the Bakerloo Line, was one of the original stations on the Baker Street & Waterloo Railway, and opened with the route on 10th March 1906. Although only a short distance from Strand, passengers walking from one to the other had to do so at street level, as, for 72 years, there was no subway connection to link them.

When completed, the Charing Cross terminus of the Jubilee Line comprised two platforms with over-run tunnels stretching some distance beyond. Cross passages led to a centralised concourse, and from here, escalators provided access to the rest of the station complex. Three of these ascended 42ft to the level of the Northern Line, whilst a similar pair, flanking a fixed stairway, climbed 33ft towards the Bakerloo.

Although a uniform style was adopted for all the new Jubilee Line stations, each one received its own distinctive platform decor. At Charing Cross, the theme was Nelson's Column and the pigeons which for so long have been associated with Trafalgar Square.

The station opened to the public on Tuesday 1st May 1979, when the erstwhile Strand was brought back into use as Charing Cross, and Trafalgar Square was similarly renamed.

When an extension of the Jubilee Line towards Stratford was mooted in the late 1980s however, it became apparent that the original link between Green Park and Charing Cross would be abandoned and replaced by new tunnels to Westminster. The section between Stratford and North Greenwich saw its first public trains on Friday 14th May 1999, and these were continued to Bermondsey four months later, during the afternoon of Friday 17th September. The following week, on 24th September, passenger services were extended to Waterloo and the final section to Green Park opened on Saturday 20th November 1999. In the small hours of that morning, at the end of Friday's traffic, the line into Charing Cross was officially closed.

The foot of the escalators leading from the upper circulating area at Charing Cross to the Jubilee Line platforms.

Works tunnel built during the construction of the Jubilee Line. (Out of view round the bend there is a right angle bend in the tunnel, at this point the works tunnel continued straight ahead to a works site under where the Sainsbury wing of the National Gallery is now located. This tunnel has now been backfilled with piles of roof panels from the Jubilee Line platforms being stored there.

SHOREDITCH

Opened: 10.4.1876
Closed: 11.6.2006

The station at Shoreditch spent much of its life as a terminus, although in its early days it was used by through services between the Great Eastern Railway at Liverpool Street and destinations south of the Thames.

It was located on the East London Railway extension which stretched northwards from Wapping and joined the GER at a junction near Brick Lane. The initial part of the ELR had opened between New Cross and Wapping in December 1869, but the northern stretch, which passed beneath the London Docks, required some careful engineering, so its completion was delayed.

Shoreditch station, along with the rest of the ELR extension, opened on 10th April 1876 and was located 37 chains north-west of Whitechapel and 9 chains east of the junction with the GER. It was entered by way of a single-storey building, tucked away on the north side of Pedley Street, but close to the better known thoroughfare of Brick Lane. Its signal box was positioned at the east end of the down platform and was built of wood. Because the junction with the GER was so close, the platforms had to be slightly staggered, with the up side lying a little west of the down.

There do not seem to have been any buildings down below, although both platforms were provided with awnings. Access from the booking hall was by means of covered stairways with that serving the down side terminating at a short enclosed walkway.

East London Line passenger services were initially worked to and from Liverpool Street by the London Brighton & South Coast Railway, but in the 1880s these were joined by trains operated by the South Eastern Railway and the GER. The ELR had long suffered from financial problems and on 10th August 1882 an Act was passed whereby the line would be leased out to five other companies. Under this arrangement it came under the joint management of the London Brighton & South Coast, South Eastern, London Chatham & Dover, Metropolitan and Metropolitan District Railways, with the GER joining in 1885.

From 1st January 1886 the LBSCR ceased to use Liverpool Street and its services were cut back to Shoreditch instead. Once the LBSCR ceased to venture beyond Shoreditch, the GER introduced its own service over the East London Line, to link Liverpool Street with New Cross and subsequently Croydon.

The street level building at Shoreditch is thought to have changed little since opening. Here it is seen in the 1930s with poster boards promoting the Underground Group, the Metropolitan Railway, the Southern Railway and the London & North Eastern Railway.

Like many inner-suburban routes, the East London Railway's fortunes suffered as a result of tramway competition and the Joint Committee took the decision to electrify the line, using the same system as employed by the Metropolitan and Metropolitan District Railways. The work was duly carried out and, after a period of trial running, electric trains began public operation on Monday 31st March 1913. From the time of electrification all passenger services were provided by the Metropolitan and those of other companies ceased. The conductor rails ended at Shoreditch, but the connection between the GER and ELR at East London Junction was retained for freight traffic and the occasional through working. The basic weekday service comprised eight local trains an hour between Shoreditch and both LBSCR and SECR stations at New Cross, although this was halved on Sundays.

Various station improvements were planned prior to electrification and Shoreditch was no exception. In May 1912, it was stated that the level of both platforms needed to be raised to 3ft above rail level. However, as the operating pattern envisaged the up side being generally used for both arrivals and departures, the down platform was removed from the scheme and the cost was reduced.

Shoreditch station seems to have gone through the First World War largely unscathed, although it was affected by an air raid incident as the conflict drew into its final year. At around 12.30am on 29th January 1918, considerable damage was caused when a bomb hit the up line, about 50 yards east of the platforms. The signalman was seriously injured and was declared unfit to work for two months, although the track was soon repaired and traffic resumed a few hours later at 7.50am.

The grouping of 1923 saw the GER being absorbed into the London & North Eastern Railway and both the LBSCR and SECR becoming part of the Southern Railway. Since 1st July 1921 the East London Line had been managed by the Metropolitan and from 1st January 1924, the 'Met' took over its maintenance. Following an Act of 1925 the ownership passed to the Southern Railway, but this had little effect on the way the route was managed, as the Joint Committee remained in place and the Metropolitan continued operation.

Early in 1915, the 'Met' had introduced a new style of platform nameboard, which comprised white lettering on a blue horizontal panel, set against a red diamond motif. Similar signs were subsequently displayed on the East London Line after 1923, although these had black lettering on a white panel, set against a green diamond, which differed in its shape from those used on the Metropolitan. Writing in the June 1953 edition of *Railway Magazine*, the late R.K. Kirkland stated that the background colour was *"a gesture to the Southern host"* and mentions that examples then remained extant at both Shoreditch and Whitechapel.

One of the 'green diamond' name signs at Shoreditch, which remained until the 1950s at least.

From 24th September 1928, the station's opening was restricted to peak hours and Sunday mornings only. In a way it was the beginning of the end.

The down platform was officially closed in 1928, but it is not known when its stairway and awning were demolished. From photographic evidence it is apparent that both were standing in January 1938, but they had gone by the late 1940s.

When the country's railways were nationalised on 1st January 1948, the line came under the British Transport Commission banner, but it was operated and managed as part of the Underground system. The East London Railway Joint Committee was finally dissolved on 2nd April 1949 and the route officially became part of London Transport.

From 24th March 1995 the East London Line was closed so that extensive refurbishment of the Thames Tunnel could take place. Originally it was intended to reopen the route in seven months, but progress was halted when the tunnel was spot listed by the Secretary of State for Heritage, before the work started.

Further delays followed and it was not until 25th March 1998 that the section linking Whitechapel with New Cross and New Cross

Shoreditch station in the 1950s, viewed from the disused down platform towards the junction with the former GER.

Gate was brought back into public use. The short stretch between Whitechapel and Shoreditch was still not ready however and a special bus service continued to operate by way of replacement. In addition to the main works, the entire line had undergone major refurbishment and the further delay was caused by unfinished signal alterations and the provision of a new buffer stop at Shoreditch. Eventually it was announced that Shoreditch would reopen on Sunday 27th September 1998 so the replacement bus service could be withdrawn.

The reopening took place as planned, but by then the station's days were numbered as the plan to extend the East London Line to Dalston Junction resulted in the need to realign the route north of Whitechapel. The scheme included replacement premises which would be provided with an all day timetable of frequent trains, so the closure could only result in giving the area a better service than before.

Closure came after traffic ceased on 9th June 2006 and engineers soon moved in and began the job of site clearance. The nameboards were removed first, followed by the stairway. Then, in March 2007, the platform awning was taken down. The platforms themselves remained a little longer but, after track lifting, the former station area was buried under heaps of spoil as the cutting was filled in. By November 2007 most of this work had been done, leaving just the street level building still standing.

The station frontage as it appeared on the afternoon of Friday 9th June 2006, its last day of use.